Instant Indonesian

How to Express 1,000 Different Ideas With Just 100 Key Words and Phrases

by Stuart Robson & Julian Millie

TUTTLE Publishing

Tokyo | Rutland, Vermont | Singapore

Published by Tuttle Publishing, an imprint of Periplus Editions (HK) Ltd.

www.tuttlepublishing.com

Copyright © 2004 by Periplus Editions (HK) Ltd.

LCC Card Number: 2003097151
ISBN 978-0-8048-3371-4

Distributed by:

Indonesia
PT Java Books Indonesia
Jl. Rawa Gelam IV No. 9,
Kawasan Industri Pulogadung, Jakarta 13930
Tel: (62) 21 4682-1088; Fax: (62) 21 461-0206
cs@javabooks.co.id

Asia Pacific
Berkeley Books Pte Ltd
61 Tai Seng Avenue #02-12, Singapore 534167
Tel: (65) 6280 1330; Fax: (65) 6280 6290
inquiries@periplus.com.sg
www.periplus.com

Japan
Tuttle Publishing
Yaekari Building 3rd Floor
5-4-12 Osaki, Shinagawa-ku, Tokyo 1410032, Japan
Tel: (81) 3 5437 0171; Fax: (81) 3 5437 0755
sales@tuttle.co.jp
www.tuttle.co.jp

North America, Latin America & Europe
Tuttle Publishing
364 Innovation Drive, North Clarendon, VT 05759-9436, USA
Tel: (802) 773 8930; Fax: (802) 773 6993
info@tuttlepublishing.com
www.tuttlepublishing.com

14 13 12 11   12 11 10 9 8

Printed in Singapore

Contents

Preface

A little language goes a long way!

It is a well-established fact that most people of average intelligence and education use a vocabulary of only five or six hundred words in going about their everyday affairs. The reason for this, of course, is that it is possible to express a variety of thoughts by using the same words in different combinations. Each additional word exponentially increases the number of thoughts one can express. Another obvious reason why a limited vocabulary is enough to get most people through the day is that they are primarily involved in basic situations that are repeated day after day.

The aim of this little book is to lay the foundation for expressing yourself in Indonesian. It will introduce 100 basic words that can be fitted together in a limited number of structures to form full sentences. Other common words are also listed, so that by substituting these in the appropriate places you will be able to say 1,000 things. And there are notes to help you when using this language in real situations.

English speakers will find it particularly easy to make basic sentences in Indonesian as the word order is generally the same as in English, there are no definite or indefinite articles or verb "to be," and no complicated rules about changing the form of words to express singular and plural or the tense of verbs.

What Is Indonesian?

Indonesian is the national language of the Republic of Indonesia. In Indonesian, it is called **bahasa Indonesia,** which just means "the language of Indonesia." Indonesian is a form of Malay, a Southeast Asian language with a long history, and is a member of a family of languages called Austronesian, which is widely spread in the Pacific region.

Before World War II, when Indonesia was still the Netherlands East Indies, nationalist leaders saw the advantages of adopting Malay as the language of the country (which they called Indonesia), as it was already widely known and had long been used for purposes of trade and administration.

As the national language, Indonesian is taught in all schools, and is used from one end of the country to the other—anywhere you go, you will be able to use it.

But Indonesian is not the only language spoken in Indonesia. In fact, there are many languages—as many as there are ethnic groups living in the various islands of the Archipelago. According to one estimate, there are 241 of these regional or ethnic languages. And some of them are quite large and important, such as Javanese (spoken in Java), with around 100 million speakers. So if you happen to be in the provinces, and find that you can't understand what's being said, it's very likely that people are using their own, local, "home" language, not Indonesian.

So the importance of Indonesian as a unifying factor is plain. This is why it is taught everywhere, and the government promotes its "good and correct" use. It is the only way people from different regions can communicate—and it is the obvious way for Indonesians and foreigners to communicate as well.

In the colonial period, Dutch was used by the elite, and many Dutch words found their way into Indonesian. These days, we find English loanwords, but please don't expect many people to speak more English than a few basic words—it's better for you to try to use Indonesian. As soon as you utter a few phrases of Indonesian, people will be delighted with your efforts, and will praise you: **Lancar sekali!** "You're very fluent!"

Indonesian is a flexible, well-developed modern language, capable of being used for any technical field, such as banking and commerce, science and technology, law and education. It has a distinctive sound: smooth and soft, sweetly flowing, without heavy stresses—the syllables tumble over each other like a babbling brook.

The national language of Malaysia, **Bahasa Malaysia**, is basically the same language as Indonesian, but there are many differences in vocabulary, so it is better not to treat them as equivalent. The differences are more than British and American English. Malay is also a regional language in some places, such as parts of Sumatra and Kalimantan, but again these varieties are by no means identical with Indonesian.

Being a national, standard language, Indonesian does not have dialects (regional variations), as other languages such as Javanese do. There are differences in pronunciation from place to place, though, because of the influence of the local language: you can hear whether a person is from Java or Bali, for example.

Jakarta is a case apart, however. The local language there is a variety of Malay, sometimes called **Bahasa Jakarta** (the language of Jakarta) or even **Dialek Jakarta** (the dialect of Jakarta). This is a very fast, lively and slangy kind of language, spoken (but not normally written) as a means of everyday communication among the inhabitants of the capital. This language became established in the course of the 19th century, and represents the form used by a range of ethnic groups, including not only the "natives" but also the Chinese and Europeans, as well as those of mixed descent, in the context of trade, the household and local administration. So the language of Jakarta is by no means identical with Indonesian as taught in school and used in the media. What people actually speak depends on what the situation is: formal or informal. The vocabulary and style are adjusted—the speaker chooses from a range of possibilities. It's clear, even in English, that slang isn't appropriate on a formal occasion, and you don't need to stand on ceremony when at home or out with friends. Someone learning Indonesian should be aware of the difference.

The Language Used in This Book

As we mentioned above, Indonesians use differing forms of Indonesian when they are in formal and informal situations. The purpose of this book is to enable you to speak as soon as possible, and so the language found in the following chapters is oriented towards the style of spoken Indonesian. This has two consequences.

Firstly, some words we will introduce to you in this book are very commonly used in spoken language, but do not appear in formal Indonesian. For example, **lagi** (in the process of) and **dikasih** (to be given) appear as **sedang** and **diberi** in the formal language. We have, however, avoided the use of slang, so you need not be concerned about offending anyone! **Lagi** and **dikasih** will not be found in situations where formal language is called for, such as formal correspondence or official speeches.

Secondly, the sentences found in this book have been created with brevity in mind. Spoken Indonesian is more economical than written Indonesian. We have left out pronouns such as "you" or "we," in sentences where you would have to use them in the equivalent sentence in English. Exactly who is being referred to should be clear from the context of the exchange. Furthermore, the device of intonation is often used to indicate meaning in Indonesian. Indonesian does have words that indicate a question is being asked, but in this book we have omitted them, and encourage you to use intonation devices, such as a rising tone, to give the impression you are asking a question.

Making Sentences in Indonesian

Every language has its own way of stringing words together to make sentences. One language finds it necessary to include (or leave out) certain items or to stress certain aspects, while another does some different way. Never expect another language to be the same as your own, in sound or construction. We all have a right to our own way of saying things.

You don't need to learn a vast number of words in order to master the elements of a language; this is the basic principle of this book. In fact the method here will be to present ***ten basic words*** per chapter, put them into various contexts, and offer some explanations. Take note of the repeated patterns in word order; knowledge of these will help you to create sentences with other words. Then together with the words found in the list at the end, you'll be able to say 1,000 things.

Pronunciation

The pronunciation of Indonesian is not difficult. After all, it doesn't have tones, as Thai, Vietnamese and Chinese do. So there's no excuse for not getting it right. Indonesian uses the roman script, and its spelling system is regular and predictable. We just have to remember what sound is represented by what letter.

Vowels

These are: *a, e, i, o, u.*

The vowel *a* is always the short sound of *ha!* — never like *ay*, or the *a* of *cat*.

The vowel *e* is mostly the short sound of the *e* of *open* or *broken*; but in a minority of cases it is different, like the *e* of *egg*. Normally there is no way of telling these two sounds apart, but in this book the second type of *e* is marked with an acute accent, *é*.

The vowel *i* is short and sharp, like the sound in *fit*.

The vowel *o* is like the *o* in *sock*.

The vowel **u** is as in *pull*, or the **oo** of *foot*, but never the long sound of *food*.

It is helpful to divide words into syllables, and to give each its full value, e.g. **ha-us** "thirsty;" **da-é-rah** "area."

Consonants

As in English, but with the following exceptions:

> **c** is always as **ch** in English *child*, never as in *cat*.

> **g** is always "hard," as in *gate*, never the "soft" **j** sound as in *germ*.

> **h** is always sounded, e.g. **sudah** "already," or **Tuhan** "God."

> **r** is also always sounded—give it a light roll.

The Alphabet

As you know, the names of letters and their sounds aren't exactly the same. And the names of the letters of the Indonesian alphabet are **not** the same as in English—they come from Dutch. It's quite important to know how to pronounce them, for example if you have to spell your name. Here is a rough guide on how to say them:

A	**ah**	K	**ka**	S	**es**
B	**bé**	L	**el**	T	**té**
C	**ché**	M	**em**	U	**oo**
D	**dé**	N	**en**	V	**fé**
E	**é**	O	**oh**	W	**wé**
F	**ef**	P	**pé**	X	**iks**
G	**gé** – hard!	Q	**ki**	Y	**yé**
H	**ha**	R	**air**	Z	**set**
J	**jé**	I	**ee**		

The most important letters to watch are A (**ah**) and R (**air** — sound the *r!*), E (**é**) and I (**ee**), because they can get confused; and also H (**ha**) and K (**ka**).

Some letters, like Q, V, X and Z, are very rare in Indonesian, and are only found in loanwords.

PART 1

Words 1–10

1 **SELAMAT** (a word used in greetings)

Selamat pagi! Good morning!

Selamat siang! Good day!
*This applies to any time in the middle of the day,
between morning and late afternoon.*

Selamat soré! Good afternoon!
*This applies to a time from late afternoon till sunset.
Note the pronunciation:* **soré**. *The* **é** *is pronounced like
the* **e** *in the English word "pet."*

Selamat malam! Good evening!

Selamat makan! Enjoy your meal!

Selamat jalan! Have a safe journey!

Selamat tidur! Have a good sleep!

From the range of expressions, you can see that **selamat** *is a general word for well-wishing. Make use of it any time, and people will be happy.*

2 APA? what?

Apa? What (did you say)?

Apa kabar? How are you?
Literally, "What news?"

Mau minum apa, Bu? What would you like to drink? (to a woman)

You will find that where English puts the "what" at the beginning of a question such as this one, in Indonesian the **apa** *comes after the verb concerned.*

Mau makan apa, Pak? What would you like to eat? (to a man)

Ada apa, Bu/Pak? What's up?; What's wrong?

Apa Indonesianya "stomach-ache?"
What's the Indonesian for "stomach-ache?"
You can put any word in place of "stomach-ache" in order to ask for its Indonesian equivalent.

3 INI this

Ini apa?/Apa ini? What's this?
The meaning is the same, but the stress is different:
the first word in the sentence gets more stress.

Ini durian. This is a durian.
You will frequently meet the simple sentence structure
illustrated by the preceding example. Note that
Indonesian does not need a word such as the English
"is"—the sentence is quite clear without it.

Ini kamar anda. This is your room.

Durian ini mahal. This durian is expensive.

Hari ini. Today.
Literally, "this day."

Pagi ini. This morning (coming, not past).

4 ITU that

Itu apa? / Apa itu? What's that?
The meaning is the same, but the stress is different:
the first word in the sentence gets more stress.

Itu siapa? Who's that?

The Indonesian says: "That is who?"

Itu isteri saya. That's my wife.

Literally, "wife of me"; in Indonesian, the thing possessed comes first, and the possessor second. This mere positioning is all that is required to express possession.

Itu mahal. That is expensive.

Itu murah. That is cheap.

5 ADA there is/are

Ada kamar? Is there a room?

In Indonesian, you will quickly find that questions are indicated not by grammatical features, but by intonation. In this example, the question would be indicated by a raised, questioning tone at the end of the sentence. The same sentence, with different intonation, would be a statement.

Ada kamar. There is a room.

Pak Tirto ada? Is Mr Tirto there?

So **ada** *can mean "to be present."*

Pak Tirto ada di rumah? Is Mr Tirto at home?

Ada. Yes, he is.

Tidak ada. No, he's not.

Ada bir? Do you have a beer?
So **ada** *can also mean "to have."*

Ada. Yes.

6 **IBU** mother; a mature woman; madam, Mrs

Ibu saya. My mother.

Ibu itu. That woman.

Ibu ada? Is your mother/wife at home?

You will have to use the words **Ibu** *and* **Bapak** *very often. The words are often abbreviated to* **Bu** *and* **Pak**. **Ibu** *should be used when addressing any woman older than yourself or whom you do not know. Younger women may be addressed as* **Mbak**, *although if you are speaking with a younger woman whom you do not know, there is nothing wrong in addressing her as* **Ibu** *also.*

Apa kabar, ibu? How are you? (to a woman)

Ibu sudah makan? Have you already eaten?

Ibu *and* **Bapak** *can have names added after them. It is not polite to use someone's name without using* **Ibu** *or* **Bapak** *before it, except with people with whom you are very familiar.*

Ibu Sri. Mrs Sri, or Sri.

Ibu Hasan sudah makan. Mrs Hasan has already eaten.

7 BAPAK father; a mature male; Mr, sir

Pak Hasan. Mr Hasan, or Hasan.

Pak Hasan sudah makan. Hasan has eaten.

Mau ke mana, Pak? Where are you going?
(to a man)

*Something that can take a little getting used to is the preference in Indonesian for using **Ibu** or **Bapak**, or even the name of a person, in sentences where English uses the pronoun "you." Speakers of Indonesian often avoid using the Indonesian equivalent of "you." Try to use **Ibu** or **Bapak** whenever you address a woman or man of the same or older age—you cannot go wrong!*

Bapak sudah makan? Have you already eaten? (to a man)

Ini kamar Bapak. This is your room. (to a man)

Pak Hasan ada kamar? Do you have a room, Hasan?

8 LAGI in the process of; still (used to express the present continuous tense)

Lagi apa, Bu? What are you doing? (to a woman)

Lagi apa, Pak? What are you doing? (to a man)

Lagi makan. Eating.

Pak Hasan lagi makan. Hasan is (currently) eating.

Bu Tirto lagi sibuk. Mrs Tirto is busy (in the middle of doing something).

Pak Tirto lagi keluar. Mr Tirto is out.

Lagi *also has another meaning, namely "more" or "again."*

9 SUDAH already

Pak Tirto sudah pulang. Mr Tirto has come home.

Anaknya sudah tidur. The children are asleep.

Sudah siap? Are you ready?

Sudah. Yes, I am.

Sudah soré. It's late (in the afternoon).

Sudah malam. It's late (in the evening).

Verbs in Indonesian are not modified to indicate tense. Instead, there are words such as **sudah** *that indicate whether an action or state has been completed.* **Sudah** *can sometimes be translated to mean "already;" it* *serves to indicate that something is completed, or already in a certain condition, and can often be translated into the English perfect tense, "has/have ...-ed." Another such word is* **belum** *"not yet":*

Sudah makan? Have you eaten?

Belum. Not yet.
You will find **belum** *very useful as a tag to end questions with:*

Pak Hasan sudah datang, belum? Has Hasan arrived, or not?

Sudah makan, belum? Have you eaten yet, or not?

10 MINTA   to ask for

Minta tolong, Pak. May I have some help? (to a male)
Literally, "I am asking for help."

Minta informasi, Pak. I am seeking information. (to a male)
The word **minta** *usually means "to ask for," but it also means "could you give me," or "I want." It is useful for making requests politely.*

Eating and Drinking

Most people love Indonesian food. But be careful of the chillis! The tiny green chillis are the hottest of all—**pedas sekali** ("very hot!"). You'll find the red chilli sauce **(sambal)** in a little jar—help yourself to just a little, to brighten things up.

What will you order? At a restaurant **(rumah makan)** you'll find a menu **(daftar makanan)**, but probably not at a food-stall **(warung)**. (The former is likely to be cleaner.) Anything with **goréng** is "fried," e.g. **nasi goréng** "fried rice."

The word **nasi** refers to rice in its cooked (i.e. steamed) form; it is the basic food of Indonesia. Almost all other dishes are usually eaten with **nasi.** Some Indonesians say that if they haven't eaten rice in a particular day, they haven't eaten! So ask for **nasi putih** "plain (literally, white) rice" with whatever you order, except with noodles and fried rice. Your fried rice will contain all sorts of tasty things, such as pieces of chicken, and should be eaten hot.

Some good tips:

➡ If there is **saté,** ask for about ten sticks. The meat may be chicken **(ayam)** or goat **(kambing)**, but never pork **(babi)** in Muslim areas. Any meat of the pig is unlikely to be served, because the pig (like the dog) is considered unclean. In Bali, however, pork is often eaten.

➡ I would recommend the **gado-gado,** mixed par-boiled vegetables such as cabbage, carrot and bean sprouts, with a tasty peanut sauce—**énak sekali** ("very nice!").

➡ If there is **nasi goréng istiméwa** (special fried rice), this usually means that a whole fried egg will be added.

What will you drink? If unsure, go for something that has been boiled. Standard is **téh manis** "sweet tea," which comes in a glass, with a neat coaster and lid. Tea is usually served with sugar already in it; so if you want tea without sugar, you should ask for **téh pahit** (literally, "bitter tea"). If you want orange juice, ask for **air jeruk**. Some people like beer **(bir)** with Indonesian food. If you just want plain water, ask for **air putih**.

By the way, the Indonesians are very proud of their fruits. Wherever you go, they will ask, "Have you tried the…?," referring to their local variety. So try to remember the name, and give it a go, and you'll find some are really delicious (and others a bit odd, like the strong-smelling **durian**).

The way to order and pay for food is generally the same everywhere, with one exception, the **Rumah Makan Padang** (Padang restaurant). In this style of restaurant, which serves characteristic, spicy food from West Sumatra, you may find the waiter piling many dishes on the table without being asked. You take food directly from the dishes, and at the end of the meal, the waiter will tally up the price of what you have eaten.

And so, **Selamat makan!** Go ahead, enjoy your meal …

PART 2

Words 11–20

11 **MAAF** (pronounced **ma-af**) sorry

The word **maaf** *is useful for excusing yourself if there is any danger that you might have done the wrong thing.*

Maaf, Pak! Sorry! (to a man)

Maaf, Ibu! Sorry! (to a woman)

Maaf, belum jelas. Sorry, I still don't understand.
Literally, "not yet clear."

Maaf, Pak, ini apa? Excuse me, what's this? (to a man)

Maaf, Ibu, sekali lagi? Excuse me, can you repeat that? (to a woman)
Literally, "once again."

Maaf, siapa nama Bapak? Excuse me, but what's your name? (to a man)

*When you are asking for someone's name, **apa** should not be used. Instead, use **siapa** "who," as in the preceding example.*

12 **PERMISI**   excuse me

Permisi, Pak, boléh lewat? Excuse me, Pak, may I get past?

13 **SILAKAN**   please, come on, go ahead

This word is usually accompanied by a hard gesture, as in the English used when the English phrase "after you" is uttered.

Silakan.   Please do; Go ahead.

Silakan duduk!   Please sit down!

Silakan masuk!   Please come in!

Silakan makan!   Please eat!
In situations in which we would merely say "please" in

English, we may need to use one of a number of Indo-nesian words. If we need help, or are asking for some-thing for our own benefit, we use **tolong** *(literally, "help") or* **minta** *(literally, "request"). But when we are inviting someone to do something for their benefit, not for ours, we must use* **silakan**, *as in the above examples.*

14 **DI** in/at/on (+ place word)

Di Jakarta. In Jakarta.

Di Jalan Asem. In Asem Street.

Di kantor. In the office.

Di depan kantor. In front of the office.

Di lantai ketiga. On the third floor.

These three little place words beginning with **s** *form a set:*

sini *means "this place, here;"*
sana *means "there (a place out of sight);" and*
situ *means "there (a place within sight)."*

Di sini. Here.

Di sana. There.

Kita makan di sini. We will eat here.

Pak Hasan masih di sana. Hasan is still there.

15 **MANA?** where?

Di mana? Where?

Kita makan di mana? Where will we eat?

Tinggal di mana? Where do you live?

Mau ke mana? Where are you going?
This is a common form of greeting in Indonesia, like "How are you?" in English. The intention is to make social contact, rather than obtain information, so feel free to give a vague answer such as **jalan-jalan** *"just taking a walk" or* **makan angin** *"just getting out and about."*

Anda berasal dari mana? Where do you come from?

16 TIDAK no, not

If you are offered a drink or food you do not want, you may simply reply **Tidak**. *It is not necessary to add a word for "thank you" to* **tidak** *in such a situation.*

Saya tidak mau. I do not intend/wish to.

Tidak ada … I do not have …/There is not …

Tidak apa. No problem./It doesn't matter.

Rumahnya tidak besar. His house is not big.

Rumahnya tidak jauh. His house is not far.
In the two preceding examples, you will notice that the particle **-nya** *is attached to the noun* **rumah**. *The function of* **-nya** *is to indicate possession by a third person (singular and plural). So,* **mobilnya** *means "his car,"* **rasanya** *"its taste."*

Mau makan, nggak? Do you wish to eat, or not?
In day to day language, you will often hear **tidak** *in the form of* **nggak.** *It is often used as a tag to end questions as in the previous example. This is an example of informal Indonesian, that is, language that is used frequently, but is not considered acceptable in the written language or formal situations.*

17 **KIRI/KANAN** left/right

Ke kiri!   To the left!

*Indonesian traffic drives on the left side of the road.
If you happen to travel on the small public buses,
which are called* **angkot, kolt** *or* **bémo** *depending on
which area you are in, you must instruct the driver in
order to stop at your desired location. You can do this
by saying, or shouting out if necessary,* **Kiri, Pak!**
(literally "left!," i.e. pull in to the kerb).

Bélok kanan di sini, Pak.   Turn right here.

Sebelah kanan.   The right side.

Langsung ke kiri!   Go immediately left!

Terus!   Continue.

Lurus!   Go in a straight line!

Setop di sini, Pak!   Stop here, Pak!

Di kiri jalan ada pasar.   On the left of the road there
is a market.

Indonesians also make frequent use of the cardinal

points to say where to go: **utara**, *north, so we could have* **dari utara**, *from the north, or* **ke utara**, *to the north; and similarly with* **selatan**, *south;* **timur**, *east; and* **barat**, *west.*

18 BERAPA how much/many?

Ini berapa? How much is this?

Ada berapa anak? How many children do you have?

Umur berapa? How old are you?

Jam berapa? What time is it?
But **Berapa jam?** *means "How many hours?"*

Harganya berapa? What is the price?

Buah ini berapa harganya? How much does this fruit cost?

Literally, "this fruit, how much is its price?" If you are concerned about the word order of the sentences you are attempting, it helps to bear in mind that there is a great degree of flexibility where word order is con-

cerned, providing you specify the relevant parts of your message clearly. The two previous examples could correctly be spoken as **Berapa harganya?** and **Berapa harganya buah ini?**

Although large retail stores in Indonesia usually offer goods at fixed prices, bargaining is expected in most other transactions. For some foreigners, bargaining is something that does not come easily, so it helps to be mentally prepared, particularly if you are unsure of the fair price for the goods you are intending to buy. Some people take the strategy of counter-offering with half of the price initially offered by the trader, then working up slowly from there. Some counter-offer with lower than half! It is up to you!

You may find it useful to take note of the environment in which you are buying. If you are buying in a location frequented by tourists, expect that the initial price will be inflated and do not hesitate to bargain hard—the trader may just be trying his or her luck! Also, if all the neighboring shops are selling similar products and it appears as though the goods are mass produced for tourists, try for a lower price. On the other hand, if you wish to purchase quality handicrafts from a location where you can observe the goods being made by skilled craftspeople, you must still bargain, but expect a higher price.

19 **HARUS** have got to/must/should

Harus bayar dulu? Must I pay first?

Harus! You must!

Saya harus pulang dulu. I have to go home (for a while).

Kamu harus sabar! You should be patient!

20 **BOLÉH** may/can/allowed to

Boléh tanya, Pak? May I ask a question?

Boléh saja. Of course you can.

Boléh tawar? Are we allowed to bargain?

Boléh makan dulu? May we eat first?

Boléh. You may.

Tidak boléh masuk. Entry is not allowed here.

Social Etiquette in Public

There are a number of social conventions relating to the body that should be borne in mind. It goes without saying that observing the behavior of others is a better method of understanding these than reading about them here! Many of these conventions are based around the concept that certain people, such as older people, are to be shown respect in a number of ways, so try to identify such people.

The right hand is preferred for eating and passing things to people. Shaking the right hand gently while smiling and bowing slightly is a polite greeting to someone you do not know, although this is not common between the sexes. A small bow with one's palms meeting in front of one's chest is polite in cross-gender introductions.

The head is the highest part of the body, and one should not touch the head of another; ruffling someone's hair as a sign of affection is not good behavior.

If you meet someone to whom you wish to show respect, such as an older person, it is good manners to try to remain below the head of that person. If that is not possible, try not to tower over them, so bow or hunch over slightly when passing. If you have to reach over someone's head, for example when passing something, then ask permission first: **Permisi ....**

As a general rule, it is polite behavior to bow over slightly and avoid walking upright when moving among seated people.

And similarly, the feet are the lowest part. It is not good manners to touch another person, or their possessions, with your feet, or point with your feet. If you are seated, the feet should not be prominently evident.

Although Indonesia is a country with a hot climate, the legs and arms are usually covered, although this differs from place to place and situation to situation. When outside of the home, the legs should be covered. This applies for males and females, although in tourist areas this is not so important; people there are used to more variety in dress styles. It is generally true that Muslim women cover their legs and upper arms in public, and this should therefore be considered a polite way for females to dress in general. When visiting mosques, it is essential to cover the arms and legs, and women should ask the attendants for advice about head covering while in the mosque.

If you go on a visit to someone's house, you will enter a sitting room at the front, probably containing a low table and a number of chairs. You should sit down closest to the entrance, facing inwards (until invited to come further), as this is the "lowest," i.e. humblest place. The host will then come out and sit facing the front. If you sit on the floor, then there will be mats, and you must take your shoes off—never tread on the mat or carpet with your shoes on.

If you are in a restaurant or elsewhere and want to draw somebody's attention, then you can beckon, but remember not to raise your hand too high and to keep the fingers pointing downwards, not upwards, in contrast to the Western method. If you have to point, it's better not to be too direct; in Java, people consider it better to use the thumb to point, rather than the forefinger.

It is also polite to not commence eating until your host or other person deserving respect has commenced. On the other hand, if you have invited people to eat with you, they will wait for you to start!

PART 3

Words 21–30

21 **KAPAN** when?

Kapan berangkat? When are we leaving? (or, When does it depart?)

Kapan datang? When did you arrive?

Kapan ke sini lagi? When will you come here again?

The English "when" can be used to refer to the happening of something in the past. **Kapan** *is not the correct Indonesian word for that sense. You should use* **ketika** *or* **waktu:**

Ketika dia datang ... When he arrived ...

Waktu mereka berangkat ... When they left ...

Visitors to Indonesia find that they are often invited to drop in to someone's house, even if they have only just

*met the person! There is a strong tradition of kindness
and respect to visitors in Indonesia, so people are keen
to invite you around to show hospitality and ask questions about your country and so on. It is a good opportunity for you to practice Indonesian and learn about
Indonesia.*

*It may be, however, that you don't have time to
visit, but find it difficult to refuse. In this situation, you
can smile and say* **kapan-kapan**. *This means "at some
unknown time in the future." This tells your would-be
host that you cannot accept the invitation at this time.*

22 TADI just now (in the recent past)

Tadi ada tamu.   Just now there was a guest.

Tadi malam ...   Last night ...

Tadi siang ...   During the day just passed ...
You will find people using the word **siang** *frequently.
It refers more or less to the period of full sunlight, and
if someone promises to come to meet you at* **siang,**
they mean during the period after **pagi** *(morning) and
before* **soré** *(late afternoon, evening).*

Tadi pagi ...   This morning ...(in the past)

23 **NANTI**   soon, next (in the immediate future)

Bapak mau makan? Would you like to eat? (to a man)

Nanti saja. Later.

Nanti kita makan di sana. We will eat there later. (shortly)

Nanti malam. Tonight. (in the night to come)

Nanti soré. This evening/late afternoon. (in the future)

24 **DEPAN**   next

Minggu depan. Next week.

Tahun depan. Next year.

25 **YANG LALU**   last (which has gone by)

The word **yang** *often functions like the English relative pronoun (who, which, that), as is clear from the above.*

You will find it useful to attach a quality to a noun. So, **mobil yang baru** *means "the car which is new," or simply "a new car."*

Tahun yang lalu. Last year.

Bulan yang lalu. Last month.

26 AKAN will, be going to

Pagi ini kami akan ke Borobudur. This morning we're going to Borobudur.
Note that the verb **pergi** *"to go" could be inserted here, but is often left out in day to day speech.*

Nanti soré akan hujan. Later this afternoon it will rain.

Bésok saya akan ke sana. Tomorrow I will go there.

In comparison with English, Indonesian is more reliant on the context of the exchange for the expression of the time at which things are to happen or have happened (tense). This will come naturally as you become more comfortable with the language. So do not be concerned about using **akan**, **lagi** *or* **sudah**, *except where these terms are essential for your message.*

Learners can sometimes be confused when seeing **akan** *in written Indonesian, as there is also a different word* **akan**, *always placed before a noun, which means "as for," or "toward." You will rarely meet this* **akan** *in day to day conversation.*

27 BERANGKAT to leave, set out

Kapan berangkat? When will you leave?

Sudah berangkat? Has he left?

You will quickly find out that it is not necessary to verbalize a pronoun or kinship term for the person you are addressing, especially in casual situations. Hence, the two preceding examples contain no indication of who is being addressed; this would be clear from the context. When you wish to indicate respect for the person you are speaking to, however, it is best to add **Bapak** *or* **Ibu.**

Pak Hasan tadi berangkat. Hasan left just now.

Berangkat ke mana? Where did he depart to?

Minggu depan saya akan berangkat. I will leave next week.

28 **PERNAH**   to have done something, already, ever

*People often use this word to ask questions with a
similar meaning to* **sudah** *(already).*

Pernah ke pasar? Have you been to the market?

Pernah. I have.

Saya pernah ke sana. I have been there.

*It is not, however, used for things that have happened
in the very recent past in the way* **sudah** *can be.*
Pernah *refers to whether something has happened
or not, with no connection to when or whether the
activity is finished. So you will certainly meet the word
if you eat with people who want to introduce you to
Indonesian food!*

Pernah makan durian? Have you ever eaten the
durian fruit?

Belum pernah. Not yet.

Dia tidak pernah bilang itu. He never said that.

29 MUNGKIN possible

Mungkin. Maybe/possibly/perhaps.

Tidak mungkin! Impossible!/No way!

Mungkin juga. Quite possibly.

30 WAKTU time

Sudah waktunya berhenti. It's time to stop.

Masih ada waktu. There's still time.

Punya waktu? Do you have time?

Waktu itu, saya belum kawin. At that time, I wasn't married yet.

Waktu itu, dia belum datang. At that time, he hadn't yet arrived.

Waktu *is not the only Indonesian word for "time." If you want to say "time" in the sense of "happening" or "occasion," you should use* **kali**, *e.g.* **satu kali** *"once" (one time),* **dua kali** *"twice" (two times), and so on.*

Times and Seasons

The days of the week are:

hari Senin   Monday

hari Selasa   Tuesday

hari Rabu   Wednesday *Also spelt*
                                Rebo.

hari Kamis   Thursday

hari Jumat   Friday

hari Sabtu   Saturday

hari Minggu   Sunday
*This **Minggu** is not to be confused with the one
meaning "week."*

The months of the year are:

bulan Januari   January

bulan Fébruari   February
*(sometimes also **Pébruari**)*

bulan Maret	March
bulan April	April
bulan Mei *(pronounced "May")*	May
bulan Juni	June
bulan Juli	July
bulan Agustus *(watch the spelling)*	August
bulan Séptémber	September
bulan Oktober	October
bulan Novémber *(sometimes also **Nopémber**)*	November
bulan Désémber	December

If you want to say "on" (a day), or "in" (a year), then you need the preposition **pada**. (**Di** is only for a physical or spatial "in/at/on," but not for time.)

For example:

Pada hari Sabtu. On Saturday.

Pada tahun 2002. In the year 2002.

The dating of years can be confusing in Indonesia, depending on where you are! The most common system is the "common era" (A.D.) used throughout Europe, but the Islamic era (A.H. **Anno Hijrah**) is also used by Muslims, and many newspapers, for example, carry the Muslim year in addition to the "common era" year. And in Bali (a Hindu society) there is yet another era, the Saka era, which is an inheritance from the Hindu period of Indonesian history; add 78 to make A.D. If you can find a Javanese or Balinese almanac, you will see how complex and interesting these calendrical systems are.

There are basically *two seasons* in Indonesia, the wet and the dry. They are termed **musim hujan** (rainy season), sometimes called **musim rendeng**, and **musim kering** (dry season), also called **musim kemarau**. The rain begins in November, reaches its height in January, and tails off in March. In the period July–September no rain is expected, and it can be very dry. It is not usual to refer to "spring" or "autumn." The "in-between" periods, around October and April, can be very sticky and hot, as there is little wind.

The rainy months are due to the prevailing wind from the west called the west monsoon or northwest called the northwest monsoon. During the dry season the wind is from the east or southeast. The dry season can be surprisingly cool at night, if there is a current of air from Australia (where it is winter at that time). Hence a jacket may come in handy. Otherwise, expect uniformly high temperatures and high humidity.

Be prepared! The seasons are one of the most common topics you will be asked about (the other is food!). So, if someone asks you about the seasons in your country, you may find these terms helpful:

Musim panas	summer (literally, the hot season)
Musim daun gugur	autumn (literally, the season of leaves falling)
Musim dingin	winter (literally, the cold season)
Musim bunga berkembang	spring (literally, the season of flowers blooming)

PART 4

Words 31–40

31 **BAGAIMANA** how? like what?

Bagaimana rasanya? What does it taste like?

Bagaimana kabarnya? How are things going?
Literally, "what is the news like?"

Bagaimana kalau kita berangkat pagi-pagi?
What do you think if we leave early in the morning?

In casual speech, **bagaimana** *may be shortened to*
gimana. Gimana *is sometimes used as a casual
greeting meaning "How are things?," to which you
may answer* **Baik** *("Good").*

32 **SEPERTI** like, as, as if

Rasanya seperti nanas. It tastes like pineapple.
Literally, "its taste is like pineapple."

Orang seperti itu … People like that …

Seperti orang Jawa … Like a Javanese person …
In this example, you will note that the word order of
orang Jawa *is the reverse of the English equivalent. In*
Indonesian, with only a few exceptions, a modifying
word comes after the word it modifies. Here are some
examples:

Rumah besar. Big house.

Orang asing. Foreign person.

Orang Belanda. Dutch person.

Seperti biasa. As usual.

33 BAIK good, okay; kind, respectable

Apa kabar? How are things?

Baik-baik saja! Just fine!

Baiklah! Okay! (I agree, let's do it)

Dia orang baik. He/she is a good person.

The opposite of **baik** *as a quality is* **buruk,** *"bad, rotten, nasty."*

34 LEBIH   more

It is used to form the comparative of adjectives ("-er, more"), e.g.:

Lebih besar.   Bigger.

Lebih baik.   Better, preferable.

Lebih énak.   Nicer (tasting, especially foods).

Lebih banyak.   More (in quantity, amount).

Lebih lama.   Longer (of time).

Lebih dulu.   Prior (before something else).

Lebih lagi.   Even more.

35 PALING   most
This word is used to form the superlative of adjectives ('-est, most"), e.g.:

Paling baik. Best.

Paling dekat. Closest.

Paling banyak. The most; at most.

Paling sedikit. The least; at the least.

36 TERLALU too (i.e. excessive)

Terlalu pedas! (This food is) too hot/spicy!
In English, we can use "hot" to mean both "hot in tem-
perature" and "spicy". Not so in Indonesian! The word
for "spicy" is **pedas,** *whereas the word for "hot*
in temperature" is **panas.**

Terlalu mahal. Too expensive.

Terlalu jauh. Too far.

Terlalu banyak. Too many.

Terlalu lama. Too long.

37 **SEKALI** very

Note that this word always follows its adjective, in contrast to **lebih, paling** *and* **terlalu**, *which come in front.*

Panas sekali. Very hot.

Mahal sekali. Very expensive.

Murah sekali! Very cheap!

Cocok sekali! Very correct!

Orang itu tua sekali! That man/woman is very old!

In Indonesian, you will notice that the gender of the person is often not specified in the particular noun or pronoun being used. The gender of the person referred to is usually clear from the context.

You will often encounter another term "very," namely **sangat**, *but this has to go in front, e.g.* **sangat berbahaya** *"very dangerous." Otherwise there is little difference.*

38 SEDIKIT a little, a bit, some

Sedikit saja. Just a little.

Anda makan sedikit saja. You eat only a little.
You will often encounter the word **saja.** *It serves to tone down and simplify the content of the utterance, in the sense of "only, just."*

Minta tambah sedikit. I would like a little more.
Tambah means "to add."

Saya pusing sedikit. I am a bit dizzy.
Pusing means "dizzy."

39 KURANG less, not enough, lacking, not very

Umurnya kurang dari tujuh belas. She is aged less than seventeen.

Uangnya kurang. The money is not enough.

Kurang bersih. Not clean (enough).

Kurang enak. Not pleasant tasting.

Saya kurang sehat. I am not so well.

In the three previous examples, **tidak** *could also be used. The difference between* **kurang** *and* **tidak,** *however, is that* **kurang** *is less strong, and so can be considered as a smoother and more polite way of expressing the negative.*

40 **LAIN** other, different

Pronounced as *la-in.*

Lain hari! Another day!

Lain kali saja! Some other time!

Note that here **lain** *comes before the word it qualifies, but in all other cases, it comes after the word it qualifies, like other adjectives, e.g.*

Orang lain. Someone else.
Literally, another person.

Yang lain. Another one.
Yang *is a very commonly encountered word, meaning "who, which, that." It can also be inserted before an*

adjective if we want to make a choice — we use **yang** *to narrow our preference to the one we desire. In this way, we can say* **yang besar** *"the/a big one" or* **yang kecil** *"the/a small one."*

Kita mencari yang lain! Let's look for another one!

Personal Pronouns

When we address people in Indonesian, it is useful to bear in mind an important difference between Indonesian and English. That is, it is common in Indonesian to use a family or kinship term instead of the Indonesian equivalent for "you."

If you wish to address a woman, for example, you can use **ibu,** the kinship term meaning "mother" or "Mrs." Of course, in English, you would rarely say to a woman "Would Mrs like a drink?" or "Would Mother like a drink?" (to someone you had just met), but in Indonesian, it is polite and correct to say **Ibu mau minum?** Similarly, you would never say in English "Does Mr wish to leave?" or "Does Father wish to leave?", but it is proper Indonesian to say **Bapak mau berangkat?**

Nevertheless, Indonesian does have pronouns also, which are set out in the table below with some notes as to usage. Note that some of the non-formal pronouns should be used sparingly with people you do not know, in order to avoid giving offence.

I, me	Non-formal:	**aku**
	Neutral:	–
	Formal:	**saya**

*Use **aku** only when talking to people you know very well or who are of the same age. Use **saya** when talking to someone who is older. If unsure, just stick to **saya**.*

you (singular)	**Non-formal:**	kamu
	Neutral:	anda
	Formal:	saudara, Bapak, etc.

Kamu *is suitable only for someone we know very well; otherwise use* **anda**, *or a kinship term or person's name with title.*

he, she, it	**Non-formal:**	–
	Neutral:	dia
	Formal:	Beliau

"He/she/they" is often not expressed, but inferred from the context. "It" or "they" is often replaced by the thing to which it refers; this is clearer, despite a tendency to repetition.

we (inclusive)	**Non-formal:**	–
	Neutral:	kita
	Formal:	–
we (exclusive)	**Non-formal:**	–
	Neutral:	kami
	Formal:	–

"We (inclusive)" includes the person you are speaking to, whereas "we (exclusive)" does not include that person.

you (plural)	**Non-formal:**	kalian
	Neutral:	–
	Formal:	Bapak-bapak, etc.

they	**Non-formal:**	–
	Neutral:	meréka
	Formal:	–

Meréka *refers only to people.*

Possession is indicated by placing the possessor after the thing possessed, but in the case of **aku, kamu** and **dia** the possessor is indicated by means of a suffix, namely **-ku**, **-mu** and **-nya** respectively, e,g. **rumahku** "my house," **mobilmu** "your car," **uangnya** "his/her money."

PART 5

Words 41–50

41 MAKAN to eat

Sudah makan? Have you eaten?

Belum. Not yet.

Ayo kita makan! Let's eat!

Mau makan apa? What would you like to eat?

Saya mau makan nasi goréng. I want to eat fried rice.

Kita makan di mana? Where shall we eat?

42 MINUM to drink

Maaf Pak, saya mau minum. Excuse me, I wish to drink. (to a man)

Mau minum apa? What would you like to drink?

Pernah minum es jeruk? Have you ever drunk **es jeruk?**

Indonesia is, of course, rich in fruits, and the juices of many fruits are drunk, sometimes in concoctions of sweets and chocolate. **Es jeruk,** *which literally means "orange ice," is actually not made directly from the juice of oranges, but from a sweet syrup with ice added. The genuine juice of the orange is known as* **jus jeruk.** *If you would like to try juice with a difference, try warm orange juice!*

Saya mau minum kopi. I would like to drink coffee.

The most commonly drunk coffee in Indonesia is boiling water poured directly over ground coffee; this is called **kopi tubruk** *(collision coffee—the water collides with the beans!). Sugar is invariably added; ask for your coffee to be* **pahit** *if you don't want sugar. There is also* **kopi susu** *(milk coffee), which has condensed milk added. Sometimes cappuccino is offered, but it may pay to check whether the establishment has a coffee machine, for these are rare outside of Jakarta and Bali.*

43 **YANG MANA** which, which one

Yang mana? Which one?

Mobil yang mana? Which car?

Mana yang lebih baik? Which one is better?

Mau makan yang mana? Which one do you want to eat?

44 **MANDI** to take a bath; to go swimming

Kamar mandi. Bathroom.

Air mandi. Water for bathing.

Bak mandi. Bathing tub.
Most bathrooms in Indonesia are fitted with a **bak mandi**. *It is a large tiled construction, something like a square tub full of water. Do not get into it! The proper way of bathing is to use the plastic scoop to splash water onto the body.*

In the countryside people bathe in a river, or at least in running water; it is impolite to approach while the bathing-place is still occupied.

Handuk. Bath towel.

45 JAUH far, distant

Jauh sekali. Very far.

Tidak jauh. Not far.

Masih jauh. It is still far.

Rumahnya jauh, tidak? Is his house far, or not?

Rumahnya jauh. His house is far.

46 DEKAT close, near

Dekat sekali. Very near.

Rumahnya dekat. His house is near.

Mana yang dekat? Which one is close?

Dekat hotel itu. Close to the hotel.

47 BAGUS good, great

Buku itu bagus. The book is good.

Buku ini tidak bagus. This book is not good.

Pakai yang bagus! Use the good one!

Ambil yang bagus! Take the good one!

Mana yang bagus? Which one is good?

48 **PADA** in, at, on

Pada hari Senin. On Monday.

Pada tanggal 4 November. On 4th November.

*Indonesian has at least two words that are equivalent to the English "in" or "at." **Pada** has a more abstract meaning compared with **di**, which applies only to physical location. **Pada** is also used in certain expressions indicating emotion felt towards someone, e.g.:*

Saya cinta pada kamu. I love you.

Saya percaya pada kamu. I trust you.

Dia bangga pada anaknya. She is proud of her son/daughter.

49 DARIPADA than, rather than, instead of

Bis lebih cepat daripada keréta api. The bus is quicker than the train.

Daripada itu … Rather than that …

Daripada itu, pakai ini! Rather than that, use this!

50 KALAU if, when; as for

Kalau hujan, jangan keluar. If it rains, do not go out.

Kalau minum kopi, saya tidak tidur. If I drink coffee, I don't sleep.

Kalau ke Bandung, naik apa? If you go to Bandung, how will you go?

Kalau saya, tidak suka.
As for me, I do not like it.

Kalau tujuh puluh lima, bagaimana?
What about seventy-five (thousand rupiah)?
Literally, "As for …, how would it be?"

Religion and Culture

Religion **(agama)** has more of a public presence in Indonesia than in many Western countries. It is quite common to be asked about your religion in public by people you may not know very well. Don't be alarmed by this; people often find this a good topic for conversation, and are usually keen to find out about a religion that differs from their own.

It is unusual for an Indonesian to not feel affiliation with one of the major established religions. The religion of some Indonesian groups is quite clear; for example, most members of Balinese society are Hindu. There are Christians in some places too. Roman Catholics are called **Katolik**, while Protestants call themselves **Kristen**. (Note that there is no general term for "Christian"—the word Kristen means "Protestant.") There are even some Buddhists. But the majority are Muslims. You will find that although most Indonesians follow Islam, there is great variety to be seen in the nature of their religious outlooks. This can be seen, at one level, in the variety of clothing people wear. Some Muslim women, for example, choose to cover their heads while in public, while others do not see this as necessary. The officially recognized religions are: Islam, Catholicism, Protestantism, Hinduism and Buddhism.

As you would expect, day to day language is influenced by Islam. A very common way of greeting people is to say

Assalamu alaikum! (Literally, May the peace of God be with you.) This is a good phrase to use if you have arrived at a friend's house and wish to notify the occupants that you are waiting at the door.

The celebration of the end of the Fasting Month (the day mostly called **Lebaran**, or more officially **Hari Raya Idul Fitri**) is a very important social occasion, especially at the family level. All modes of transport are overbooked at that time, as people travel home in order to be with the family and ask forgiveness of the elders (**Maaf lahir batin**) for any misdemeanors they may have committed. The date of this holiday moves back 10 days each year, as it of course follows the Islamic calendar.

Visitors will note the large number of mosques in cities and towns, as well as in the countryside, and will hear the call to prayer five times daily, broadcast by loudspeakers. During the Fasting Month, there may be recitation during the night as well (**taravéh**). The volume may be a surprise, especially early in the morning for dawn prayers, but after you leave Indonesia you may miss the call, as the recitation of the Arabic text has a distinctive sound.

PART 6

Words 51–60

51 **NAIK** to go by (a means of transport); to go up

Kita naik apa? How will we go?
Literally, "What will we go on?"

Kita naik keréta api. We will go by train.

Pak Hasan sudah naik, belum? Has Hasan already
got on/boarded?

Dia naik pesawat terbang ke Makasar.
She went by airplane to Makasar.

**Meréka naik keréta api dari Bandung ke
Yogyakarta.** They went by train from Bandung to
Yogyakarta.

52 **HABIS** finished, all gone, expired

Uang saya habis. I am out of money.

Uangnya belum habis. His money has not yet run out.

Karcisnya sudah habis! The tickets are all gone!

Habis is a very common word in the spoken language. You will hear people use this word in many situations with the meaning of "after...."

For example:

Habis makan, kita ke setasiun. After we finish eating, we will go to the station.

53 MASUK to go into, to enter

Silakan masuk! Please come in!

Dilarang masuk! It is forbidden to enter!

Pak Hasan sudah masuk hotélnya. Hasan has gone into his hotel.

Masuk forms part of many idioms:

Tidak masuk akal. It makes no sense./It's unreasonable.

Masuk sekolah. To attend school.

Masuk kantor. To be at the office.

Masuk angin. To have a chill.

Masuk Islam. To become a Muslim.

54 **BICARA** to speak, talk

Bapak/Ibu bisa bicara bahasa Inggeris? Can you speak English?

Saya ingin bicara dengan Pak Hasan. I would like to speak to Hasan.

Boléh saya bicara dengan Pak Hasan? May I speak with Hasan?

Dia sedang bicara. He is speaking with someone.

Sebelum pergi, bicara dengan Pak Hasan dulu. Before you go, first speak with Hasan.

55 **TANYA** to ask

Boléh tanya, Pak?   May I ask a question, Pak?

Tanya di informasi saja!   Ask at the information desk!

Remember that when you ask a stranger a question, it pays to show politeness in the tone of your voice and body language. It can sometimes be disconcerting for a person to be asked for help by a foreigner, so bow-ing the head slightly, smiling, and speaking slowly with a gentle tone will make it easier for the person from whom you are seeking assistance to understand your question.

Don't forget, if you are asking for something for your own benefit, the correct word to use is **minta.**
Minta tolong, Bu?   May I ask for your help?
(to a woman)

56 BESAR large

Rumah itu besar.   That house is big.

Saya mau yang besar.   I want a big one.

Bir besar, atau bir kecil?   A large beer? Or a small one?

Di sebelah rumah besar itu.   Next to the big house.

57 KECIL small

Rumah itu kecil. That house is small.

Saya mau yang kecil. I want a small one.

Kamar kecil. Toilet.

Di depan warung kecil itu. In front of the small food stall.

58 MELIHAT to see

Sudah melihat Monas, belum? Have you seen the national monument?

Mau melihat Gunung Merapi? Do you want to see Mount Merapi?

Affixes are often added to words to provide additional meanings. **Lihat** *is very often used in the form* **kelihatan,** *meaning "visible" or "it seems."*

Here are some examples:

Gedung itu kelihatan. The building can be seen.

Kelihatannya, Pak Hasan sudah masuk. It seems Hasan has already gone in.

59 RASA taste; feeling, sense

Rasanya asin. It tastes salty.

Rasanya manis. It tastes sweet.

If you are a person who likes to drink tea, you should realize that traditions concerning this drink differ from place to place in Indonesia. In some places, it is taken for granted that tea is drunk sweet, often with a number of spoonfuls of sugar. Bottled tea usually has a large amount of sugar added. So, if you want tea with no sugar, ask for **téh pahit** *(literally, bitter tea). It is not traditional to drink tea with milk in Indonesia, although hotels will of course serve milk with tea if requested. Nevertheless, some of the tea varieties drunk in Indonesia are delicious without milk, so give them a try first!*

Rasanya pedas. It tastes hot!

Saya rasa ... I feel/think/am of the opinion ...

60 MAHAL expensive

Harganya mahal. It is expensive.
Literally, its price is expensive.

Mahal sekali, Pak/Bu! That's very expensive!
Some people find it hard to get into the spirit of bargaining with a trader when buying something. You may find the phrase **Mahal sekali, Pak/Bu!** *useful as your first reply to the seller after he tells you his starting price. It will tell the seller that you intend to pay less than what he has asked for. Don't forget to inject horror and surprise into your voice! It doesn't matter if you sound insincere, for a dash of theatrics or humor can add friendliness to the bargaining process.*

Social Chatting

The topic of a person's place of origin is a polite and interesting way to start a conversation in Indonesian. Perhaps because Indonesia has so many diverse ethnic groups and cultures, people find it interesting to talk about origins (**asal**) and places they have been to or heard about. It is not rude to ask about someone's origin. Taxi drivers in Jakarta, for example, usually come from outside Jakarta, from Java or Sumatra, for example. Their wives and children often continue to reside in their home towns. This kind of travelling for work is called **rantau**.

So, if you want a simple and failsafe way to start up a conversation, try the following:

Bapak dari mana? Where are you from? (to a man)
Where are you coming from?

Or,

Ibu asalnya mana? Where do you come from? (to a woman)

Another popular conversational topic is family. In general, in Indonesian custom, it is not impolite to ask someone about their marital status, or the number of children they have.

You may be invited into a person's home, even by a person you may have only just met. They may say:

Mampir dulu! Please drop in!
Literally, drop in first.

There are two possibilities here. If a person wishes to go home, and you are near their house, their invitation for you to come in may well be a polite formality only. On the other hand, it will often happen that a person would genuinely like you to visit and have a chat in the front reception room that all Indonesian homes—no matter how small—are equipped with. Being a foreigner, you will find that people will be interested in details about your home country and your own situation. It is a strong tradition in Indonesia to treat visitors with warmth and respect.

If someone has achieved something, e.g. got a degree, had a child, become engaged, and so on, then you can say simply **Mengucapkan selamat** or just **Selamat!** This means literally "I express the wish 'may you enjoy good fortune'," that is, "Congratulations!" It is all-purpose.

The word **selamat** can be used when wishing someone well with any sort of undertaking, e.g. **Selamat belajar** "Best wishes with your study;" or **Selamat makan** "Enjoy your meal;" or **Selamat jalan** "Have a safe journey."

When you meet a new friend, and want to introduce yourself (or introduce someone else to them), you just say **Kenalkan**, and mention your name: **Nama saya** … "My name is … ."

When it's time to go, you should take leave properly, by saying **(Saya mau) minta diri**, meaning "I ask permission (to go)." Your host will answer **Mari!** which here just means "Goodbye!" The phrase **Saya pulang dulu** "I am going home now," can also be used as an introduction to a polite departure.

PART 7

Words 61–70

61 **SAMPAI** up to; to arrive

Pak Hasan sudah sampai, belum? Has Hasan arrived yet?

Surat anda belum sampai. Your letter has not yet arrived.

Bis malam sampai di Jakarta jam berapa? What time does the night bus arrive in Jakarta?

Sudah sampai ke mana? How far have you come? *You will make great use of this construction, as it can refer not only to distance travelled, but also to progress in the abstract sense, such as that of plans, projects and so on.*

Saya belum sampai ke sana. I haven't arrived at that point yet.

62 KASIH to give

Uangnya sudah dikasih, belum? Has the money been given yet?

Itu sudah dikasih. That has already been given.

Saya dikasih uang seratus ribu. I was given 100,000 (rupiah).

*In the previous three examples, the prefix **di-** has been added to the base word. This has the effect of making the verb passive. That is to say, **kasih** (to give) becomes **dikasih** (to be given, is given). You will find this prefix is very common, and that the passive form is used frequently in situations in which you may not expect it.*

63 KETEMU to meet

Kapan ketemu sama Pak Hasan? When did you meet Hasan?

Baru ketemu. We have only just (i.e. recently) met.

Saya ketemu Pak Hasan di términal bis. I happened to meet Pak Hasan at the bus station.

Sampai ketemu lagi! Till we meet again!/See you later!

64 BARU new; only recently, only just, only then

Ini mobil baru. This is a new car.

Pak Hasan baru datang. Hasan has just arrived.

Saya baru sembilan bulan di sini. I have only been here for nine months.

Saya baru dari Médan. I have only just come from Medan.

65 BELAJAR to study; to learn

Saya belajar bahasa Indonesia. I am studying Indonesian.

Saya harus belajar lagi. I must do more study.

Tolong Pak, saya mau belajar bahasa Indonesia. May I ask your help? (to a male) I wish to study Indonesian.

Boléh belajar sama saya. You may/can study with me.

66 MALU to act shyly, with reserve, dignity and propriety; embarrassed, ashamed.

Jangan malu! Don't be shy!

Dia dibikin malu. He was embarrassed./He lost face.

Kalau di mesjid, harus malu. If you go to a mosque, you should act with reserve.

Saya malu minta tolong. I was ashamed to ask for help.

As you can see from these examples, **malu** *means more than the English "shy." It is a social concept concerned with "keeping face" and proper behavior. Even if people you associate with do not express* **rasa malu** *(feelings of* **malu***), it is beneficial and interesting to observe how people react in particular social situations. For example, when meeting an old person, people may often act with a reserve that they may not show towards other people.*

In general, reserve in speech and body language indicates respect.

67 BENAR right, correct, true; proper

Itu benar! That is correct!

Bisnya berangkat jam sepuluh, benar? The bus leaves at ten o'clock, right?

Kabar itu tidak benar. That news is not correct.

*In the three examples above, the word **betul** can be used in place of **benar**.*

Dia orang benar. He is a virtuous person.

68 TUNGGU to wait

ruang tunggu waiting room

Tunggu di sini! Wait here!

Tunggu sebentar. Wait for a moment.

Saya tunggu di mana? Where should I wait?

Tunggu di hotél. Wait in the hotel.

69 BUAT for; to do; to make

Buat apa? What for?

Ini buat siapa? Who is this for?

Buat semantara. For the time being.

If we add the prefixes **mem-** *or* **di-** *to* **buat,** *it has the meaning "to make."*

Harus membuat yang baru. I must make a new one.

Ini baru dibuat. This has only just been made.

70 JANGAN don't, let's not

Jangan malu! Don't be shy!

Jangan kencing di sini. Don't piss here.

Jangan sampai terlambat! Don't be late!

Social Relations and Family

Learners of Indonesian need to know a number of guidelines concerning social relations that have implications in day to day language.

The terms **bapak** and **ibu** deserve special attention. In an abbreviated form, namely **Pak** and **Bu,** they serve as titles before names, like "Mr" and "Mrs." They are used much more than the English "Mr" and "Mrs," and show that we recognize the person's social status. In conversation, they are used before the name of the person being addressed; to use the bare name, without **ibu** or **bapak,** would suggest a degree of intimacy that would be improper in most cases.

One guideline that may take some getting used to is the use of a kinship term rather than the Indonesian equivalent of "you." This guideline helps you to avoid giving offence.

Here is an example:

Bapak mau minum apa?

This translates literally as "Mr would like to drink what?," but is a polite way of saying "What would you like to drink?" to a male of older age or a similar-aged male with whom we are not familiar. Notice the Indonesian does not require a word for "you."

Here is another example:

Ibu baru datang, betul?

Literally, this means "Mrs has only just arrived, correct?" It is polite Indonesian for "Have you just arrived?" when speaking to an older female or a similar-aged female with whom we are not familiar.

Similarly, people sometimes use their name or kinship title in place of "I" or "me." This is similar to the English construction "Do as Mummy (= I) tells you." So, do not be confused if your friend Tono, wishing to say "I have not been there," says:

Tono belum pernah ke sana.
Tono has not been there.

Finally, you will note that some kinship words, in fact, have no gender distinction. You can address a younger male or female with **adik,** and an older male or female with **kakak.** This latter term, however, should only be used with someone with whom you are very familiar. Apart from their use as terms of address, the words **adik** and **kakak** are also nouns, meaning "younger sibling" and "older sibling" respectively.

PART 8

Words 71–80

71 **HIDUP** life; to be alive; to be in operation

Ibunya masih hidup. His mother is still alive.

ACnya hidup, belum? Is the air-conditioning on yet?

AC is pronounced **a-sé.** *If you wish to check whether a vehicle or room has air-conditioning, you should ask* **AC ada?** *"Does it have air-conditioning?"*

Hidup di Jakarta mahal. Living in Jakarta is expensive.

72 **PUNYA** to have

Punya uang kecil? Do you have any small change?

Punya seribu. Silakan! I have a thousand rupiah. Please, go ahead!

You will find that small change is handy in daily life, especially when it comes to paying the parking controllers. Treat them well! You will rely on them to watch over your car when parked, and to help you to break into traffic upon leaving, especially in the larger cities!

Punya istri, belum? Do you have a wife yet?

Sudah. Anak saya dua! I do. (*Literally, "already"*) I have two children!

73 **HARI INI** today

Hari ini, mau ke mana? Where do you want to go today?

Hari ini, saya mau ke bank! I want to go to the bank today.

Hari ini hari apa? What day is it today?

Hari ini hari Selasa. Today is Tuesday.

Ada tur hari ini? Is there a tour today?

Tidak ada hari ini. Bésok saja. Not today. It is tomorrow.

74 MAU to want; to intend to; to be about to

Tidak mau! I don't want to!/I don't want that!

Mau makan nasi? Do you want some rice?

Tidak. Sudah makan. No. I've already eaten.
It is not common or necessary to say the equivalent of the English "No, thank you." **Tidak** *is quite okay.*

Mau yang kecil, atau yang besar? Do you want a small one or a big one?

Saya mau yang besar. I want a big one.

75 SAKIT sick

Saya sakit. I am sick.

Pak Toni sakit hari ini. Toni is sick today.

Pak Toni sakit apa? What is wrong with Toni?

Anak saya sakit! Ada dokter di sini? My child is
sick! Is there a doctor here?

76 HARGA price, value

Berapa harganya? How much is it?

Harganya delapan puluh ribu rupiah. Its price is
eighty thousand rupiah.

Ada korting? Is there a discount?

Harga mati. Fixed price.

Mobil itu, berapa harganya? What's the price of
that car?

77 HILANG to disappear, to vanish, to be lost

Paspor saya hilang! My passport has disappeared!

Uang saya hilang! My money has disappeared!

Lucy kehilangan jam tangannya. Lucy lost her
watch.

78 **MATI** dead, deceased

Pak Hasan mati. Hasan is dead.

Orang tuanya mati, belum? Are his parents dead yet?

ACnya mati. The air-conditioning is off.

Harga mati. Fixed price

79 **URUS** to manage, to organize

Tolong, Pak. Minta mengurus visa saya? May I ask your help, sir? Could you please handle my visa?

Bisa diurus di sini? Can it be handled here?

Perpanjangan visa sulit diurus. A visa extension is hard to arrange.

Bu Noto lagi mengurusi anak-anak. Bu Noto is currently looking after the children.

Bukan urusanmu! It's no business of yours!

80 **BUKAN** isn't it? (used to form tag questions); not (with nouns)

This is generally placed at the end of the sentence, and invites the answer "yes;" that is, it asks for confirmation.

Ini términalnya, bukan? This is the terminal, isn't it?

Términal ini besar, bukan? This terminal is big, isn't it?

Note that in speech **bukan** *is often shortened to* **kan**.

Términal itu jauh sekali, kan? The terminal was a long way, wasn't it?

Bukan *is also used to negate nouns.*

Dia bukan mahasiswa. He is not a student.

Bukan urusanmu! It's no business of yours!

Indonesian Names

The Indonesian naming system varies somewhat from region to region. In many Muslim areas you will see that a man has two names: the first is his own, and the second is his father's. For example, with **Nafron Hasyim,** this man is **Pak Nafron** (not **Hasyim**); his father was **Hasyim**. In other words, the name is in fact "Nafron son of **Hasyim**." In some other countries one will see the word **bin** used here, meaning "son of." Pak Nafron's wife is just called **Bu Nafron**.

In Java men mostly have only one name—to the bafflement of foreigners, who expect a surname and a given name. However, they do have a childhood name, which is replaced by the adult name. Names are changed without formality. A girl too has a childhood name, not normally used after she marries. If a person is a Christian, you will see initials, standing for the baptismal names (e.g. F.X. for **Franciscus Xaverius,** or M.I. for **Maria Immaculata**).

The system in Bali is very complicated, because of its Hindu "caste" system, involving various titles for Brahmins, royalty and nobility. Ordinary people, the majority, have the title **I** (not an initial!), followed by a title indicating their birthorder in the family, as follows: **Wayan**, **Madé**, **Nyoman**, and **Ketut**—and if there are more, you go back to **Wayan**.

Indonesians, especially in official life, make much use of titles. People with academic degrees like to indicate their degree with **Dr** (**doktor**, not **dokter**) for a PhD, or **Drs**

(doktorandus) and **Dra (doktoranda)** for a male and female respectively who have passed the preparatory examination for a doctorate. Military people have their titles according to rank, and within the Javanese aristocracy there are also many different grades with appropriate titles.

PART 9

Words 81–90

81 PESAN order, reservation; to order, reserve, book

Sudah pesan, belum? Have you ordered yet?

Pesan apa, Pak? What [food] would you like to order, sir?

Pesan saya nasi goréng sama jus jeruk.
My order is fried rice and orange juice.

Karcisnya sudah dipesan, belum?
Have the tickets been ordered yet?
As explained at word number 62, the prefix **di-** *is often added before a verb, such as occurs in this example. It is used to indicate the passive voice, so* **dipesan** *means "to be ordered." Your meaning will usually be clear no matter which voice you use, so do not be concerned about making mistakes in this regard. Nevertheless, with experience, you will pick up certain situations in which the passive voice is used.*

A further note about ordering; tipping is not necessary, although it is, of course, much appreciated.

82 BAYAR to pay

Mbak! Kita bayar di mana? Where can we pay?
When addressing waiters, you have a choice. If the waiter is younger than yourself, you may use **mas** *(brother, friend) for males, and* **mbak** *(miss) for females. Nevertheless, if the waiter or waitress is older, or if you just feel more comfortable using a term bearing more respect for the addressee,* **pak** *and* **bu** *can be used.*

Di kas, Pak. At the cashier, sir.

Bon ini sudah dibayar! This bill has already been paid!

83 MENUKAR to exchange

Saya perlu menukar uang. I need to change some money.

Di mana bisa menukar uang? Where can I change money?

Bapak mau menukar apa? What do you wish to exchange?

Saya mau menukar dolar AS dengan rupiah.
I am going to exchange US dollars for rupiah.
AS (United States) is pronounced **a-és.** *Note that the qualifying word comes after the word it modifies. In English we say "US dollars," whereas in Indonesian we say* **dolar AS.** *In the same way, "fried rice" is* **nasi goreng** *(rice fried).*

Kalau menukar di jalan, harus hati-hati! If you exchange in the street, you must be careful!

84 MENGIRIM to send

Saya ingin mengirim kartu pos. I wish to send a postcard.

Berapa ongkosnya untuk mengirim surat ke Australia? How much does it cost to send a letter to Australia?

Mau dikirim léwat pos udara? Do you want it to be sent by airmail?
This is another example of the use of a passive voice.

*The reasons for the addition of the letter **k** after the **di-** prefix are explained at the end of this part.*

Saya mau mengirim pakét ini dengan pos kilat.
I want to send this package by express post.

85 KENAL acquainted

Sudah kenal? Do you know (that person)?

Kita belum kenal. We have not been introduced.
*Remember that **kita** includes the addressee, so this sentence is equivalent in meaning to "you and I have not been introduced."*

Kita sudah kenal. We know each other.

Saya kenal sama dia. I know him.

86 SURAT letter, document

Surat kilat. Express letter.

Surat kilat khusus. Special delivery.

Surat kabar. Newspaper.

Surat ini dari Pak Hasan. This letter is from Hasan.

87 MAIN (pronounced "**ma-in**") to play

Main suling/piano/trompét. To play the flute/
piano/trumpet.

Main tennis/voli/bulutangkis. To play tennis/
volleyball/badminton.

Dia main-main saja. She's just playing
(not serious).

Main ke rumah, ya? Come round and pop in, okay?

88 PAKAI to wear; to use

Pakai apa, Pak? What will you use? (to a man)

Pakai keréta api. I will take the train.

Pakai gula, Bu? Do you take sugar? (to a woman)

Kita pakai bahasa Indonesia, ya? We will use
Indonesian, okay?

Saya lebih suka pakai bahasa Inggris. I would prefer to use English.

89 AMBIL to take

Mau ambil pakaian, Pak. I wish to take my clothes. (to a man)

Sudah diambil. They have already been taken.

Ambil yang mana, Pak? Which one will you take? (to a man)

90 PAS a good fit, suitable; exact(ly), precise(ly)

Pas! Just right!

Uang pas. Correct money, the exact amount.

Sepatu ini pas. These shoes are a good fit.

Pas di depan rumahnya. Right in front of his house.

Pas-pasan. Just enough to get by.

Verb Prefixes

Me- *prefix*

Of the words above, two begin with **me-**, namely **menukar** and **mengirim**. If we attempt to find these words in the dictionary, we will not find them under the letter *m*. This is because the words are arranged in the dictionary according to a base word; in these cases, the base words are **tukar** and **kirim**.

Many verbs in Indonesian have such a prefix affixed to them. In fact, the words **pesan**, **ambil**, **bayar** and **pakai** are all used frequently in the affixed form. Here is how they change:

Pesan becomes **memesan**.

Ambil becomes **mengambil**.

Bayar becomes **membayar**.

Pakai becomes **memakai**.

How do we know the correct form of this **me-** prefix? The form follows the initial letter of the root word. The rules are summarized in the following table on page 99:

Initial letter of base word	Form of the prefix me-
Any vowel, *h*, *g*, *kh*	**meng-**
r, *l*, *y*, *w*	**me-**
m, *n*, *ny*, *ng*	**me-**
k	**meng**, *k* is deleted
p	**mem**, *p* is deleted
s	**meny**, *s* is deleted
t	**men**, *t* is deleted
d, *c*, *j*, *z*	**men-**
b, *f*, *v*	**mem-**

What difference does the prefix make? In general, you will find that the prefix must be added to a number of words if they take an object. In other words, most verbs with the prefix **me-** are transitive. Another goal of adding the prefix is to make an intransitive verb from an adjective.

Do not worry about whether you should use a prefixed form or not!! Firstly, your meaning will almost certainly be clear even if you use the incorrect form. Secondly, many prefixes tend to be omitted in day to day language, so nobody may notice if you happen to use the less correct form.

Di- *prefix*

As stated above, the **di-** prefix is very commonly used in Indonesian, and it has the effect of making a verb passive. Hence:

Mengirim. To send.

Dikirim. To be sent.

The reason why the letter *k* appears in the passive form is that the root word of **mengirim** is **kirim.** When the **di-** prefix is added, there is no change to the word such as those that take place when the **me-** prefix is employed. **Di-** is simply added to the root word.

PART 10

Words 91–100

91 **TÉLÉPON** telephone

Ada télépon, Pak? Is there a telephone here?
(to a man)

Tidak ada télépon. Pakai wartel saja! There is no
telephone. Use the wartel!

*Many homes in Indonesia do not have telephones.
However, each neighborhood usually has a* **wartel**
(warung télékomunikasi) *where calls can be made to
various destinations. For the duration of your call, the
cost is displayed on a small screen. Don't be confused
between* **wartel** *and* **warteg!** *A* **warteg (warung
Tegal)** *sells characteristic food from Tegal, in Central
Java!*

Saya mau télépon. I want to use the telephone.

Lagi sibuk. The telephone is busy.

92 **TINGGAL** to live; to remain; to leave

Tinggal di mana? Where do you live?

Saya tinggal di Jalan Acéh. I live in Aceh Street.

Tinggal satu. There is one left.

Meninggal dunia. To pass away.

93 **SIAP** ready, prepared

Sudah siap, belum? Are you ready yet?

Pak Hasan belum siap. Hasan is not yet ready.

Kita harus siap pada jam sepuluh. We must be ready at ten o'clock.

Pakaiannya belum siap, Pak. The clothes are not yet ready, Pak.

94 **MENJADI** to become

Sudah menjadi mahal. It has become expensive.

Cuaca menjadi panas. The weather's getting hotter.

Dia menjadi guru. He is a teacher.

The word **jadi** *is frequently used at the beginning of a sentence, indicating a consequence:*

Jadi, Pak Hasan tidak mau. So Hasan is not willing.

Jadi, kita tidak berangkat. So, we did not leave.

95 LAKI-LAKI male, man

You will have noticed that pronouns in Indonesian usually indicate age rather than gender. **Laki-laki** *is used where it is necessary to specify that the person concerned is male.*

Seorang laki-laki. A male person.

Adik laki-laki. Younger brother.

There are other words for male; the sign indicating the gentleman's toilet will usually read **pria** *(male).*

96 PEREMPUAN female, woman

This word is used to specify female gender.

Seorang perempuan. A female person.

Adik perempuan. Younger sister.

The ladies' toilet is indicated by **wanita** *(female).*

97 DAPAT to get, to obtain; to be able, to have success

Dapat? Did you get it? Were you successful?

Sudah dapat tikétnya, belum? Have you got the tickets or not?

Belum dapat. I have not yet got them/been able to get them.

Maaf Pak, tidak dapat di sini. I am sorry, that cannot be done here.

98 DICUCI to be washed

Sudah dicuci, belum? Have (the clothes) been washed?

Pakaiannya lagi dicuci. The clothes are being washed.

Pakaiannya belum dicuci. The clothes have not yet been washed.

If you wish to ask someone to do your washing, or to arrange for it to be done, there are a number of ways of asking. The most polite, and this is appropriate if you are staying in a private home, is to ask:

Tolong Bu, ini bisa dicuci? May I have your help, could these possibly be washed?

Other ways of asking are:

Ini bisa dicuci? Can these be washed?

Minta dicuci, Pak. Please have these washed. (To a man)

99 SELESAI finished, completed

Sudah selesai, belum? Is it finished yet?

Pakaiannya belum selesai. The clothes are not yet finished.

Kita berangkat sebelum selesai. We left before it was finished.

100 CINTA love

*This can be of various kinds: towards one's little brothers/sisters (**adik-adik**), parents (**orang tua**), homeland (**tanah air**) or, of course, boyfriend/ girlfriend (**pacar**).*

Jatuh cinta. To fall in love.

Aku cinta padamu. I love you.
*You will find that pronouns are often abbreviated and added to other words, possibly to indicate possession, or possibly to indicate the object of a preposition. The word **padamu** is formed by adding **-mu,** which is an abbreviation of **kamu** (you), to the preposition **pada** (to).*

Numbers

The Indonesian numeral system is very simple and regular. Numbers are ranged from large to small, without the use of "and." Having learned the words for "one" to "ten," apart from a special term for the "teens," any number can be formed, simply using the counting words **puluh** ("tens"), **ratus** ("hundreds"), and **ribu** ("thousands"). Note that **se-** is a form of satu, "one."

0	**nol**
1	**satu**
2	**dua**
3	**tiga**
4	**empat**
5	**lima**
6	**enam**
7	**tujuh**
8	**delapan**
9	**sembilan**
10	**sepuluh**
11	**sebelas**
12	**dua belas**
13	**tiga belas**
14	**empat belas**
15	**lima belas**

16	**enam belas**
17	**tujuh belas**
18	**delapan belas**
19	**sembilan belas**
20	**dua puluh**
21	**dua puluh satu**, *etc.*
30	**tiga puluh**
40	**empat puluh**
50	**lima puluh**
60	**enam puluh**
70	**tujuh puluh**
80	**delapan puluh**
90	**sembilan puluh**
100	**seratus**
200	**dua ratus**
300	**tiga ratus**, *etc.*
1,000	**seribu**
2,000	**dua ribu**
10,000	**sepuluh ribu**
100,000	**seratus ribu**
1,000,000	**sejuta**

For example:

25	**Dua puluh lima**
161	**Seratus enam puluh satu**
2002	**Dua ribu dua**

Note that in Indonesian the decimal point is indicated with a comma, and the thousands marked with a dot.

Ordinals

Ordinals are formed using the prefix **ke-** attached to a numeral, which then follows the word qualified, like an adjective, e.g. "the fifth child" **anak yang kelima**. Some people say **anak nomer lima** "child number five."

However, this does not apply to dates. We say **tanggal empat belas Novémber** for "the fourteenth of November."

Fractions

Fractions are formed using the prefix **per-** attached to a number, and preceded by an indication of how many, e.g. "three quarters" **tiga perempat**, "nine tenths" **sembilan persepuluh**.

In connection with measures, for "half" we use **setengah**, e.g. "half a kilo" **setengah kilo**, "half an hour" **setengah jam**. But without the measure, then the word is **separuh**, e.g. "Half of it's used up!" **Separuhnya habis!**

Telling the time

Jam berapa? What time is it?

Jam satu. One o'clock.

The word **pukul** *is also used instead of* **jam,** *but is more formal.*

For "past" we say **léwat** *or* **lebih,** *e.g.:*

Jam dua belas léwat sepuluh. Ten past twelve.

Jam enam lebih lima. Five past six.

Jam lima léwat seperempat. A quarter past five.

For "half" we say **setengah,** *but this is half to the next hour, e.g.:*

Setengah sembilan. Half past eight.

Setengah tiga. Half past two.

For "to" (= before), we say **kurang** *("less"), e.g.:*

Jam delapan kurang seperempat. A quarter to eight.

Jam satu kurang enam menit. Six minutes to one.

The twenty-four hour clock is also used, for example in airline schedules, e.g.

Pukul dua puluh dua, empat puluh. 22.40

Emergency Expressions

Nanti dulu! Just a moment!

Sebentar, ya! One moment, please!

Bagaimana? Pardon?

Maaf? Excuse me?

Jangan! Don't (do that)!

Bukan! No! (It's not like that.)

Ada apa? What's up?

Maaf! Sorry!

Permisi! Excuse me! (Let me pass, etc.)

Lain kali saja! No, thanks. (Some other time.)

Tidak apa-apa. I don't mind. (It's okay.)

Biarlah. I don't care. (Leave it.)

Boléh tanya? May I ask you something?

Minta bantuan. Could you help me?

Tolong! Help!

Tak mungkin! No way!

Cukup! That's enough! (No more!)

Anu, ... By the way, ...
Omong-omong, ...

Terserah. It's up to you. (Please yourself.)

Baiklah! Okay. (I agree, let's do it.)

Bagus! That's great!

Apa boléh buat! What can you do?!

Awas! Look out!

Masa! Really?! (I don't believe it.)

Mari! Come on! (Let's go!)

Sekali lagi? Could you say that again?

Hati-hati! Be careful!

Kebetulan! What a coincidence! (How lucky!)

Sayang sekali! What a pity! (How unfortunate!)

Syukurlah! Thank heavens!

Some Common Signs about Town

Awas copét. Beware of pickpockets.

Satu arah. One way.

Jalan buntu. No through traffic.

Jalan pelan-pelan banyak anak.
Drive slowly, many children.

Jangan kencing di sini. Don't urinate here.

Awas anjing galak. Beware of the dog.

Tamu harap lapor. Visitors must report.

Dilarang masuk. No entry.

Harap antri. Please queue up.

Harap tenang. Please be quiet.

Patuhi tanda-tanda lalu lintas. Obey traffic signs.

Bélok kiri jalan terus. Free left-hand turn.

Additional Vocabulary

Note that when verbs are formed with the prefix **me-**, first the base word (which is usually used in everyday conversation) is given in bold, then the prefixed form (which is usually used in formal, written language) is given in bold within parentheses. A slash indicates alternative forms.

A

a mostly untranslated. To specify "a, one" use a counting word like **satu**; for large and medium-sized objects, **sebuah**; for people, **seorang**

able to, can **bisa**

about (approximately) **kira-kira;** (concerning) **tentang/mengenai**

according to **menurut**

account, bill **rékening**

accuse, to **tuduh (menuduh);** accusation **tuduhan**

accustomed, used to **biasa/terbiasa**

acquainted, to be acquainted with **berkenalan dengan;** acquaintance **kenalan**

act, to (in a … way) **berbuat;** (noun)**perbuatan**

add, to **tambah (menambah);** addition **tambahan**

addict **pecandu**

address, to address (a letter) **alamat (mengalamatkan);** (noun) **alamat**

admire, to **kagum (mengagumi);** admiration **kekaguman**

advance, to (go forward) **maju**

advice **nasihat**; to advise **menasihati**; adviser **penasihat**

after **sesudah/setelah**; after that, from then on **sesudah itu/ selanjutnya**

afternoon **sore**

again **lagi**; once again **sekali lagi**

age **umur**; aged **berumur**; (formal) **berusia**; for ages **lama sekali**

agency **agén**

agenda **acara**

agree, to **setuju**; to agree to something **menyetujui**; to agree to, be so kind as to **berkenan**

agriculture **pertanian**

air-conditioning **AC** (pronounced ah-sé)

aircraft **pesawat**

airline (company) **perusahaan penerbangan**

airmail **pos udara**

alive **hidup**

all **semua**; all of it **semuanya**

alley **gang**

along **sepanjang**

already **sudah**

also **juga**

although **walaupun**

always **selalu**

amazed **héran**; amazing **menghérankan**

ancient **kuno**

and **dan**

angry **marah**; anger **kemarahan**

announcement **pengumuman**

another **(yang) lain**

answer, to **jawab (menjawab)**; (noun) **jawaban**

ant **semut**

anything **apa-apa**

apparently (it looks as if…) **rupanya**; (it turned out that …) **ternyata**

appreciate, to **harga (menghargai)**; appreciation **penghargaan**

arrange, to (organize, manage) **urus (mengurus)**; to organize, take care of **mengurusi**; manager **pengurus**; management **pengurusan**

arrive, to **sampai/tiba**; arrival **kedatangan**

arrogant **sombong**; arrogance **kesombongan**

art **kesenian**

article (written) **artikel**

as (in the capacity of) **sebagai**; (because) **karena**; (as if) **seperti**; (as for) **kalau**

ask, to ask for **minta**; (a question) **tanya/ bertanya**; to ask about **tanya (menanyakan)**; to ask someone for something **minta (memintai)**

asleep, to be asleep **(sudah) tidur**; to fall asleep (unintentionally) **tertidur**

aspiration **aspirasi**

assist, to **bantu (membantu)**; assistance **bantuan**; (household) assistant **pembantu**

at **di**; **pada**

ATM **ATM** (pronounced ah-té-em)

atmosphere (surroundings) **suasana**; (air) **hawa**

attend, to (be present at) **hadir (menghadiri)**

attention **perhatian**; to pay attention to **hati (memperhatikan)** *attitude* **sikap**

attract, to **tarik (menarik)**; attractive **menarik**

audible **kedengaran**

aunt **bibi**; (Westerner) **tante**

B

back (rear) **belakang**; (of body) **punggung**

backpack **ransel**; backpacker **turis ransel**

backward, neglected **tertinggal**

bad (quality) **buruk**; (character) **jelék**

badminton **bulutangkis**; badminton player **pemain bulutangkis**

bag **kantong**; (handbag) **tas**

baggage **bagasi**

Balinese **Bali**; (language) **bahasa Bali**

bank **bank** (pronounced bang)

bargain, to **tawar (menawar)**

base, basis **dasar**; to have a base **berdasar**; to base something on **mendasarkan**; to be based on **berdasarkan**; to form the base of **mendasari**; basically **pada dasarnya**

bathe, to (have a bath) **mandi**; to bath **memandikan** See also "swim"

bathing cap **topi renang**; bathing place **tempat mandi/ permandian**

bathroom **kamar mandi**

batik **batik**

battery **bateré**; (car) **aki**

be, to be there **ada**

beach **pantai**

bear, to bear in mind **mengingat** See also "stand"

beautiful (of nature) **indah**; beauty **keindahan** See also "pretty"

because **karena**; because of **oléh karena**

become, to **jadi (menjadi)**

bed **tempat tidur**; bedspread **seperéi**

beer **bir**

before (first) **sebelum**; (formerly) **dulu**

beggar **pengemis**

begin, to **mulai**; beginning **permulaan**

behavior **kelakuan**

bench, seat **bangku**

beside **di samping**

best **paling baik**; it would be best to … **sebaiknya**

better **lebih baik**

bid, offer **tawaran**

big **besar**

bill, account **rékening**

birth, to give birth **lahir (melahirkan)**

birthday **hari ulang tahun**

bitter **pahit**

black **hitam**

blanket **selimut**

blocked (jammed, traffic) **macet**

blow, to **bertiup**; **tiup (meniup)**; to blow away **terbang (menerbangkan)**

blue **biru**

board, panel, council **déwan**; board of directors **déwan pengurus**

bone **tulang**; fishbone **duri ikan**

book **buku**

booking, to make a booking **membooking**

border **perbatasan**; to border on **berbatasan dengan**

bored **bosan**; boring **membosankan**

born, to be born **lahir**

bottle **botol**

bottom **bawah**

box **kotak**

boxing **tinju**; boxer **petinju**

boy **anak laki-laki**; boyfriend **pacar**

brain **otak**

break, to break down (car refuses to go) **mogok**

brick **batu mérah**

bright (light) **terang**; (colour) **cemerlang**

broadcast, to **siar (menyiarkan)**; (noun) **siaran**

broken (not working) **rusak**

brokenhearted **patah hati**

brother (younger) **adik**; (elder) **kakak** (add **laki-laki** for male gender only if required)

brown **coklat**

browse (look around), to browse **lihat (melihat-lihat)**

bucket **émbér**

build, to **bangun (membangun)** building **bangunan**, (large) **gedung**

bus **bis**; night bus **bis malam**

business (affair) **urusan**; (firm) **perusuhaan**

busy **sibuk**; (got something else to do) **ada acara;** (crowded, noisy) **ramai**

but **tapi**; (more formal) **tetapi**

buy, to **beli (membeli)**

by (following a passive verb) **oléh**

bye! **dah!**

C

call, to call in **mampir**; to call someone **panggil (memanggil)**; to be called (have the name…) **bernama**

campus **kampus**

can, able to **bisa/dapat**

cancelled **batal**; to cancel **batal (membatalkan)**; cancellation **pembatalan**

capable of **dapat**

car **mobil**

careful **hati-hati**

carriage (car of train) **gerbong**

carry, to **bawa (membawa)**; something carried **bawaan**; to carry out (run, execute) **laku (melakukan)**

cash **kontan**; to cash (cheque) **tukar (menukarkan)**

cashier **kas**

cause **sebab**; to cause **sebab (menyebabkan)**

celebrate, to **raya (merayakan)**; celebration **perayaan**

ceremony **upacara**

certain(ly) **pasti**

chair **kursi**

change, to (intransitive) **berubah**; (transitive) **ubah (mengubah)**; (replace, exchange) **ganti (mengganti)**; (noun) **perubahan**; (money) **uang kecil**

chase, to **kejar (mengejar)**; to chase time, keep up, lose no time **mengejar waktu**; to chase each other, play chasing **kejar-kejaran**; caught up with **terkejar**

chat, to **bercakap-cakap**

cheap **murah**

chicken **ayam**

child **anak**; (respected person's) **putra**

chill, to have a chill **masuk angin**

chilli **cabai** (pronounced cabé); (sauce) **sambal**

chook **ayam**

choose, to **pilih** (**memilih**); choice **pilihan**

circumcision **sunatan**

citizen **warganegara**

city **kota**

claim (insurance); to make a claim **menclaim** (note spelling)

class (school) **kelas**; middle school **golongan menengah**

classical **klasik**

clean **bersih**; to clean **bersih** (**membersihkan**)

clear (easy to understand) **jelas**; (weather) **terang**; to clear (letterbox) **angkat** (**mengangkat**)

clever (intelligent, mentally agile) **cerdas**; (bright, gifted) **pandai**; (skilful, adroit) **cakap**

climate **iklim**

climb, to (mountain, hill) **daki** (**mendaki**)

clock **jam**

close **dekat**

close, to **tutup** (**menutup**); to be closed **tutup**

cloth **kain**; piece of cloth (for wiping) **lap**

clothes, clothing **pakaian**

cloudy, overcast **mendung**

coast **pantai**

coat, jacket **jas**

coconut (palm) **pohon kelapa**; (fruit) **buah kelapa**; coconut milk **santan**

coffee **kopi**

coincidence, by **kebetulan**

cold **dingin**; to feel (too) cold **kedinginan**; to have a cold **kena pilek**

colleague **rekan**

colonial **kolonial**

color **warna**; colored **berwarna**

come, to **datang**; Come on! **Mari!**; to come in **masuk**

commemorate, to **ingat (memperingati)**

compile (compose, write) **karang (mengarang)**; (arrange) **susun (menyusun)**

completely, (not) at all **samasekali**

concept, idea **gagasan**

conclusion, to draw a conclusion **menarik kesimpulan**

condition **keadaan**

condolences I offer my condolences **turut berdukacita**

confront, to (bring face to face) **hadap (menghadapkan)**

connect, to (transitive) **hubung (menghubungkan)**; connection **hubungan**; in connection with **berhubungan dengan**, **berkenaan dengan**; (to connect, telephone) **sambung (menyambung)**; connection **sambungan**

conscience **hati kecil**

consider, to (regard) **anggap (menganggap)**

consist, to consist of **terdiri dari**

contain, to **berisi**; contents **isi**; to have as contents **berisikan**

continually **terusmenerus**

contribute, to **sumbang (menyumbang)**; contribution **sumbangan** *convey, to* (pass on) **sampai (menyampaikan)**

cool **sejuk**

corner **pojok**

correspond, to (exchange letters) **bersurat-suratan**

corruption **korupsi**

cotton **katun**

countenance, face **wajah**

course **kursus**; intensive course **kursus inténsif**

course, of **tentu saja**

crammed, crammed full **penuh sesak**

cross, to (intransitive) **seberang (menyeberang)**; (transitive) **(menyeberangi)**

cruise ship **kapal pesiar**

cup **cangkir**

cupboard **lemari**

custom (habit) **kebiasaan**; (tradition) **adat**; to go through customs **meliwati duane**

cut, to **potong (memotong)**; something cut off (reduction, discount) **potongan**

D

daily, a day/per day **sehari**

dance, to **tari (menari)**; (noun) **tarian**, dances in general **tari-tarian**

daring, audacious, brave **berani**; audacity, bravery **keberanian**

date (of month) **tanggal**; (agreement to meet) **janji**

daughter **anak perempuan**

day **hari**

daytime **siang**

dead **mati**

dean **dékan**

decent, proper **pantas**

decide, to **putus (memutuskan)**; decision **keputusan**

declaim, to **déklamasi (mendéklamasi)**

declaration (written statement) **surat keterangan**; tax declaration **surat fiskal**

deep **dalam**; depth **dalamnya**

deficiency **kekurangan**

degree (of temperature) **derajat**; (academic) **gelar**

delayed **mengalami keterlambatan**

dengue fever **demam berdarah**

depart, to **berangkat**; departure **keberangkatan**

deputy, representative **wakil**

develop, to (intransitive) **berkembang**; (transitive) **kembang (mengembangkan)**; development **perkembangan, pengembangan**

dictionary **kamus**

differ, to **berbéda**

difference **perbédaan**; (deviation) **kelainan**

different **lain**; (from each other) **berlainan**

difficult (hard, complicated) **sulit**; (hard to deal with) **sukar**; difficulty **kesulitan, kesukaran**

diligent **rajin**; diligently **dengan rajin**

diminish, to **turun (menurun)**

direct(ly) **langsung**

direction **arah**

dirty **kotor**; dirt **kotoran**

disappointed **kecéwa**; disappointing **mengecéwakan**; disappointment **kekecéwaan**

discount **potongan**

discover, to (find, come across) **temu (menemukan)**

discuss, to **bicara (membicarakan)**; discussion **pembicaraan**

district (area, region) **daérah**

disturb, to **ganggu (mengganggu)**; disturbance (noise, etc.) **gangguan**; (riot) **kerusuhan**

dive, to (from board, etc.) **terjun**; (underwater) **selam (menyelam)**

dizzy, headachy **pusing**

do, to (act) **berbuat**

doctor (medical) **dokter**

dollar **dolar**

don't **jangan**; don't let … **jangan sampai**

door **pintu**

down (to the bottom) **ke bawah**

down-payment **persekot**

drain **got**

drink, to **minum**; (noun) **minuman**

drive, to (car) **kemudi (mengemudi)**

drop, to drop in (call in) **mampir**; (to let fall) **jatuh (menjatuhkan)**

drug (medicine) **obat**; drugs (narcotics) **narkotika**

drunk **mabuk**

dry **kering**; dry season **musim kering/ kemarau**; to dry (transitive) **kering (mengeringkan)**; to dry (transitive) (in the sun) **jemur (menjemur)**

Dutch **Belanda**; (language) **bahasa Belanda**

E

early (in the morning) **pagi**; (in the afternoon) **siang**; (in the evening) **sore**; earlier (before others) **lebih awal**, (formerly) **dulu**

earring **subang**

east **timur**

eat, to **makan** See also "food"

economy, economic **ékonomi**

electricity, electric **listrik**

elephant **gajah**

else, what else **apa lagi?** who else **siapa lagi?**

embarrassed **malu**

emergency **darurat**

emphasise, to (give priority to) **penting (mementingkan)**; (lay stress on) **tekan (menekankan)**

employee, personnel **pegawai**

empty **kosong**

enclosure, pen, stall **kandang**

engaged (to marry) **bertunangan**; (busy, phone line) **sedang bicara**

engine-driver **masinis**

English **Inggeris**; (language) **bahasa Inggeris**

enjoy, to **nikmat (menikmati)**; enjoyment **kenikmatan**

enough **cukup**

enter, to (intransitive) **masuk**; (transitive) **memasuki**

era **jaman**

especially **terutama**

even (laying stress) **pun**; even though **biarpun**

event, incident **peristiwa**

ever, once **pernah**

every, each **tiap**

everyday (usual) **sehari-hari**

everyone **semua orang**

everywhere **di mana-mana**

everything **segala-galanya**

evidence, proof **bukti**

exact, the exact amount **uang pas**; exactly **tepat**

exaggerated, excessive **berlebihan**

examine, to **periksa (memeriksa)**; examination (investigation) **pemeriksaan**; (school) **ujian**

except **kecuali**

excess, surplus **kelebihan**

exchange, to **tukar (menukar)**

excuse, to **maaf (memaafkan)**; excuse me **permisi**

exist, to **ada**

expand, to (intransitive) **berkembang**; (transitive) **kembang (mengembangkan)**

expenses, costs **ongkos**

expensive **mahal**

experience, to **alam (mengalami)**; (noun) **pengalaman**

explain, to **terang (menerangkan)**; explanation **penjelasan**

express, to (pronounce) **ucap (mengucapkan)**; expression **ucapan**

express (post) **pos kilat**; (train) **keréta api eksprés/cepat**

extend, to (transitive) **panjang (memperpanjang)**; extension **perpanjangan** *extra,* something added **tambahan**

extraordinary **luar biasa**

F

face (noun) **muka**

face, to (intransitive) **hadap (menghadap)**; (transitive) **menghadapi**

fact, in fact, actually **sebenarnya**

fading, hazy, obscure **kabur**

faint, to **pingsan**

fall, to **jatuh**

family **keluarga**

fan **kipas angin**

far **jauh**

fare (bus, taxi) **tarif**

farmer **petani**

fast **cepat**

fast, to **berpuasa**

fasten, to (belt) **kena (mengenakan)**

fat **gemuk**

father **bapak**, (formal) **ayah**; Father (RC priest) **romo** (NB "o" as in English "got", not "go")

favorite (most liked) **kesenangan**

feel, to (emotion) **rasa (merasa)**, (sensation) **terasa**; feeling **perasaan**

female **perempuan**

fever **demam**

fiancé(e) **tunangan**

field (open space) **lapangan**

fill, to **isi (mengisi)**; full **berisi**

film, movie **filem**

finally **akhirnya**

find out, to **ketahu (mengetahui)**

finished (done) **selesai**; (used up) **habis**

fire (general) **api**; (house, etc.) **kebakaran**; to play with fire **main api**

fireworks (decorative) **kembang api**; (crackers) **petasan**

first (before something else) **dulu**; (in order) **pertama**

fit, to (intransitive) (clothes) **pas**; (transitive) **mengepas**; fitting room **kamar pas**

flight **penerbangan**

flirt, to (make eyes) **main mata**

flute **suling**

fly, to **terbang**; to fly over **menerbangi**; to fly in all directions **beterbangan**; to cause to fly, blow away **menerbangkan**

fly (insect) **lalat**

follow, to (intransitive) **berikut**; (transitive) **ikut (mengikuti)**

food **makanan**

foot **kaki**

football **sépak bola**; footballer **pemain sépak bola**

for (on behalf of) **untuk**, **buat**; (with length of time) **selama**; (with thanks) **atas**

force, to **paksa (memaksa)**; (noun) **paksaan**; forced, obliged **terpaksa**

forget, to (intransitive) **lupa**; (transitive) **melupakan**; forgetful **pelupa**

fork **garpu**

found, to (set up) **diri (mendirikan)**

frank, candid **terus terang**

friend **teman/kawan**; boy/girlfriend **pacar**

friendly **ramah-tamah**

frightened **takut**; frightening **menakutkan**

from **dari**; (with times) **mulai**

front **depan**; at the front **di depan**; in front (facing) **di hadapan**

fruit **buah**; (fruits, in general) **buah-buahan**

fry, to **goréng (menggoréng)**; fried **goréng**

full **penuh**

funny **lucu**

fussy, troublesome **réwél**

G

gamble, to **berjudi**; gambling **perjudian**; gambler **tukang judi**

gas **gas**

gate **gerbang**

gather, to (intransitive) **berkumpul**; (transitive) **kumpul**

(mengumpulkan); gathering **kumpulan**

gaze, to **pandang (memandang)**; to gaze at **memandangi**; (noun) **pandangan**

general, common **umum**; generally **umumnya**

gents (toilet) **priya**

get, to (obtain) **dapat (mendapat)**; (become) **jadi (menjadi)**

gift **hadiah**; (brought home after a trip away) **oléh-oléh**

girl (female child) **anak perempuan**; (unmarried) **gadis**; girlfriend **pacar**

give to **beri (memberi/ memberikan)**

glass (for drinking) **gelas**; (in window, mirror) **kaca**

go to **pergi**; to go by (means of transport) **naik**; to go up **naik**; to go in **masuk**; to go down **turun**

goat **kambing**

good **baik**; good morning **selamat pagi** (and so on)

goods, articles, objects **barang-barang**

goodbye, to say goodbye **minta diri**

grade (school) **kelas**

great (wonderful) **bagus**; (big) **besar**; (famous) **termasyhur**

green **hijau**

greet, to **salam (menyalami)**

greetings **salam**

grey **kelabu**

group (of people) **rombongan**

guess, to (estimate) **duga (menduga)**; (noun) **dugaan**

guess, to (think) **kira (mengira)**

guest **tamu**

H

hair **rambut**

half (with a measure) **setengah**; (with a quantity) **separuh**

hand **tangan**

happen, to (occur) **terjadi**; (go ahead) **jadi**; happening **kejadian**

happy **senang**

hat **topi**

hate, to **benci pada**; (noun) **kebencian**

have, to **ada**; (more formal) **punya (mempunyai)**

have, to (must) **mesti**

he **dia**; (respectful) **beliau**

head **kepala**

headcloth (men's) **destar**

healthy **séhat**; health **keséhatan**

hear, to **dengar (mendengar)**; can be heard **kedengaran**

heart (seat of emotions) **hati**; (anatomical) **jantung**

heavy (weight) **berat**; (rain) **lebat**

help, to **tolong (menolong)/bantu (membantu)**; (noun) **pertolongan/ bantuan**

her **dia**; (respectful) **beliau**; (possessive) **-nya**

here (in this place) **di sini**; (to this place) **ke sini**

hill **bukit**

him **dia**; (respectful) **beliau**

hire, to (rent) **séwa (menyéwa)**

his (suffix) **-nya**

hold, to **pegang (memegang)**; to hold hands **berpegangan tangan**

home **rumah**; at home **di rumah**; to feel at home **kerasan**; to go home **pulang**

homeland **tanah air**

honest **jujur**; honesty **kejujuran**

hope, to **harap**; to hope for **harap (mengharapkan)**; (noun) **harapan**

hope, I hope (may you …) **mudah-mudahan**

hospital **rumah sakit**

hot (temperature) **panas**; (chilli) **pedas**; to be too hot (suffer from the heat) **kepanasan**

hotel **hotel**

hour **jam**

house **rumah**

how? **bagaimana?**

how much, how many? **berapa?**

hug, to **peluk (memeluk)**; to hug each

other **berpeluk-pelukan**

human being **manusia**

humid **lembab**; humidity **kelembaban**

hundred **ratus**; one hundred **seratus**

hurt, to **sakit**; to be hurt (injured) **luka**; (offended) **tersinggung**

husband **suami**

I

I, me **saya/aku**

ideal (dream) **cita-cita**

if **kalau**

illuminate, to **terang (menerangkan)**; illumination **penerangan**

imitate, to **tiru (meniru)**; imitation **tiruan**

immediately **segera**

impatient **kurang sabar**

important **penting**; importance **pentingnya**

impression **kesan**; impressive **mengesankan**

in **di**

included **sudah masuk**

increase, to (intransitive) **bertambah**

inform, to (let know) **beritahu (memberitahu)**

information **keterangan**; for your information **untuk informasi**

informed (knowledgeable) **maklum**

initiative **inisiatif**

inside **di dalam**

instant (moment) **saat**

instructions (directions) **petunjuk**

insurance **asuransi**

intention **maksud**; to intend **bermaksud**

interested **tertarik**; interesting **menarik**

interior (hinterland)
pedalaman

internet café **warung internét, warnét**

introduce, let me **kenalkan**

irrespective, regardless **tak pandang bulu**

Islam **agama Islam**

island **pulau**

isn't it? **bukan**

it (translation depends on context; often not translated)

itch(y) **gatal**

J

jackfruit **nangka**

Javanese **Jawa;** (language) **bahasa Jawa**

join, to join in **ikut**

joke **lelucon**

just (recent past) **baru;** just enough **pas-pasan**

just (fair) **adil;** justice **keadilan**

K

kangaroo **kanggaru**

keep, to (put away, store) **simpan (menyimpan);** (remain in good condition) **tahan lama**

kind, sort **macam**

kind, kind-hearted **baik hati**

knee **lutut**

knife **pisau**

know, to (understand) **tahu** (pronounced ta-u); knowledge **pengetahuan**

know, get to know **kenal**

L

lacking, not enough **kurang**

ladies (toilet) **wanita**

lake **danau**

lamp, light **lampu**

land (ground) **tanah**; (arable area) **lahan**

lane (passage between houses) **gang**

language **bahasa**

large **besar**; on a large scale **besar-besaran**

last (past, gone by) **yang lalu**; (in order) **yang terakhir**

late (behind schedule) **terlambat**; (in the morning) **siang**; (in the afternoon) **soré**; (at night) **jauh malam**; later **belakangan**; later on, in future **kelak**; the late **almarhum**

laugh, to **tertawa**; to laugh at **tawa (menertawakan)**; laughter **tawa**

lay, to (place, put) **letak (meletakkan)**

lead, to **pimpin (memimpin)**; leader **pemimpin**; leadership **pimpinan**

leave, to (set out) **berangkat**; to leave behind **tinggal (meninggalkan)**

lecture (university) **kuliah**

left (not right) **kiri**

left, to be left (remain) **tinggal**; left behind by accident **tertinggal**

leg **kaki**

let, let's **mari kita** …; let it be **biarlah**; let me **biar saya**; to let (allow) **biar (membiarkan)**

letter **surat**; express letter **surat kilat**; special delivery letter **surat kilat khusus**; letter of introduction **surat pengantar**; registered letter **surat tercatat**; to send a letter to someone **surat (menyurati)**

letterbox **bis surat**

licence (driver's) **SIM (surat izin mengemudi)**

lie (to lie down) **berbaring**; (to be located) **terletak**; (to tell lies) **bohong**

life **kehidupan**

like (resembling) **seperti**

like that **begitu**; like this **begini**

like, to **suka**; would like to… **mau**

line **baris**

list **daftar**

listen, to listen to **dengar (mendengarkan)**

little **kecil**; a little, a bit **sedikit**

live, to **tinggal**

location **letak**; located **terletak**

lodgings (small hotel) **losmén**

lonely, deserted **sepi**; to feel lonely **kesepian**

long **panjang**; (of time) **lama**

longing, yearning **rindu**; to long for, miss **rindu (merindukan)**

look, to look at **lihat (melihat)**; to look for **cari (mencari)**; to look alike **mirip**

lose, to lose something **kehilangan**

lost (gone) **hilang**; (to have lost the way) **tersesat**

lot, a lot **banyak**

love **cinta**; to love **cinta pada/mencintai**; love letter **surat cinta**; to fall in love **jatuh cinta**; to love each other **bercinta-cintaan**; loved, beloved **tercinta**; would love to **ingin sekali**

M
Madam **Bu**

mail **pos**

main (road/street) **jalan besar**

majority **kebanyakan**

make, to **buat (membuat)**; making, manufacture **pembuatan**; maker **pembuat**; to make (appoint) **jadi (menjadikan)**

male **laki-laki**

manager **ménéjer**

mango **mangga**

mangosteen **manggis**

manuscript **naskah**

many **banyak**

market **pasar**

marks (for school work) **angka**

married **kawin**, (formal) **nikah**

match (sport) **pertandingan**; (for lighting) **korék api**

mathematics **matématika**

may (allowed) **boléh**; (perhaps) **mungkin**

me **saya**

meaning **arti**

meat **daging**

medicine **obat**; (herbal medicine) **jamu**

meet, to **bertemu dengan**; (to go to meet) **temu (menemui)**; (go and fetch) **jemput (menjemput)**; (catch up with) **ketemu**

memory **ingatan**; memories **kenang-kenangan**

mention, don't mention it (you're welcome) **kembali**; to mention something **sebut (menyebutkan)**

menu **daftar makanan**

method, way **cara**

middle **tengah**

Middle East **Timur Tengah**

milk **susu**; cow's milk **susu sapi**

mind **hati**; of like mind **sehati**; to mind (object)

berkeberatan; to mind (watch over) **jaga (menjaga)**

minibus (intercity) **travel**

minute (noun) **menit**

mistake **kesalahan**

moment, a moment **sebentar**; in a moment **sebentar lagi**

monument **tugu**

moon **bulan**; moonlight **terang bulan**; full moon **bulan purnama**

morning **pagi**

money **uang**

money-belt **sabuk uang**

month **bulan**

more (with adjective) **lebih**; (with time) **lagi**; (not) any more **tidak ... lagi**

mosque **mesjid**

mosquito **nyamuk**; mosquito coil **obat nyamuk**

most **paling**

mother **ibu**

motorcycle **sepéda motor**

mountain **gunung**

much **banyak**

Muslim **Muslim**; a Muslim **orang Muslim**; to become a Muslim **masuk Islam**

must (have to, got to, should) **harus**

my **saya** (placed after noun)

N

nail polish **cat kuku**

name **nama**; family name **nama keluarga**; first name **name kecil**

napkin (table napkin, serviette) **serbét**

narrow **sempit**

nation **negara**

nationality **kewarganegaraan**

nature, natural **alam**

nauseated **jijik**; nauseating **menjijikkan**

necessary **perlu**

need, to **perlu**; to need something **butuh (membutuhkan)**

neglected **terlantar**

neighbor **tetangga**; neighboring (near by) **berdekatan**

never **belum pernah**

new **baru**

news **kabar**; news report **berita**

newspaper **surat kabar/ koran**

next (coming, in time) **depan**; (in order) **yang berikut**

night **malam**

no **tidak**, (colloquial) **ndak, nggak**

noise, sound **bunyi**; noisy **bising**

nonsense **omong kosong**

north **utara**

not **tidak**, (colloquial) **ndak, nggak**; not yet **belum**; not very **tidak begitu, kurang**; (before a noun or pronoun) **bukan**

note, to **catat (mencatat)**; (noun) **catatan**; noting, registration **pencatatan**

nothing, it's nothing **tidak apa-apa**

notice, to take notice of **hati (memperhatikan)**

notification (call to attend) **surat panggilan**

novel **roman**

now **sekarang**

numb (to go to sleep, e.g. leg) **semutan**

number (telephone, flight, etc.) **nomer**; (total)

jumlah; a number of (some) **sejumlah**; (digit) **angka**

O

objection **keberatan**; to have an objection **berkeberatan**

obtain, to (get) **dapat (mendapat)**

o'clock **jam**, (formal) **pukul**

odd, strange **anéh**

office **kantor**

often **sering**

old (aged) **tua**; (former) **lama**

omelette **dadar**

omitted, left out **ketinggalan**

on (position) **di**; (time) **pada**

on (running, going) **hidup**

once (one time) **sekali**; (formerly) **pernah**

one **satu**

onion **brambang**

only, just **saja** (placed after)/**hanya** (placed in front)

only (not before) **baru**; only now **baru sekarang**

open **buka**; to open **buka (membuka)**; (outgoing) **terbuka**; opening hours **jam buka**

opinion **pendapat**; to be of the opinion that … **berpendapat bahwa**

opportunity **kesempatan**; to have the opportunity to **berkesempatan**

opposite to, facing **berhadapan dengan**

orange **jeruk**

order, to (reserve, book) **pesan (memesan)**; (noun) **pesanan**

order, out of order **rusak**

organization **organisasi**

origin **asal**; to originate, come from **berasal dari**

other **lain**

our **kita** (inclusive of you), **kami** (exclusive of you) NB placed after the object possessed

out, to be out **sedang keluar**

outside **luar**, **di luar**

outstanding **tonjol (menonjol)**

over, to take over **mengambil alih**

over (the road, river) **di seberang**

overseas **luar negeri**, (formal) **mancanegara**

own, to **punya (mempunyai)**; (one's) own **sendiri**

P

paid, settled **lunas**; to pay off, settle (debt) **lunas (melunasi)**

palace **istana**; (Javanese) **kraton**; (Balinese) **puri**

pale **pucat**

parcel, package **pakét**

pardon? **maaf?**

parent(s) **orang tua**

part **bagian**; a part of **sebagian**

part, to (intransitive) **berpisahan**; parting **perpisahan**

participate, to participate in **ikut serta dalam**; participant **peserta**

party, celebration **pésta**

pass, to (hand) **beri (memberikan)**; to pass (go by) **léwat (meléwati)**; to pass (exam) **lulus**; to pass away **meninggal (dunia)**

passenger **penumpang**

passport **paspor**

past (beyond, in times of day) **léwat**

patient **sabar**; patience **kesabaran**

patient (noun) **pasién**

pay, to **bayar (membayar)**; payment **bayaran**

peanut **kacang**

pedicab **bécak**

pension **pensiun**

people, national group **bangsa**

performance **pertunjukan**

period **jaman**; the Majapahit period **jaman Majapahit**

permanent(ly) **tetap**

person (man, woman) **orang**

petrol, gasoline **bénsin**

piano **piano**

pickpocket **copét**, (formal) **pencopét**; to have one's pocket picked **kecopétan**

picnic, excursion **tamasya**

pig, pork **babi**

pile, stack, heap **tumpuk**; to stack up **tumpuk (menumpuk)**

pillow **bantal**

pineapple **nanas**

pink **jambon, mérah muda**

pity, what a pity! **sayang sekali!**

place **tempat**

plan **rencana**; to plan **rencana (merencanakan)**

plane **pesawat terbang**

plate **piring**

plateau **dataran**

platform (railway) **péron**

play, to (general, musical instrument, sport) **main**; to play (show, present) **main (memainkan)**; to play around **main-main**; player **pemain**

please, kindly (formal request) **harap**; (inviting someone) **silakan**

pleasing **senang (menyenangkan)**

pocket **saku**; pocket money **uang saku**

poetry **puisi**

point, to **tunjuk (menunjuk)**; to point out, demonstrate **menunjukkan**

politics, political **politik**

poor **miskin**; poverty **kemiskinan**

porter (uniformed) **portir**; (general) **kuli**

position, status **kedudukan**

possess, to **punya (mempunyai)/milik (memiliki)**

possession **milik**; possessor **pemilik**

possible, possibly **mungkin**; possibility **kemungkinan**

post, position **jabatan**

postcard **kartu pos**

postcode **kode pos**

post office **kantor pos**

postpone, to **tunda (menunda)**; postponement **penundaan**

practice, to **latih (melatih)**; practice **latihan**

precisely **presis**

prefer, to **lebih suka**

present, to be present **hadir**; to be present at **hadir (menghadiri)**

present, gift **hadiah**

pretend, to (feign) **buat (membuat-buat)**

pretty **cantik**; prettiness, beauty **kecantikan**

price **harga**; fixed price **harga mati**

principal (head) **kepala**; (main) **utama**

probably **boléh jadi**

problem, question **soal**; there's a problem (something stopping me) **ada halangan**

programme (TV, radio) **acara**

progress, to **maju**; (noun) **kemajuan**

prohibit, to **larang (melarang)**

promise **janji**; to make a promise **berjanji**; to promise something **janji (menjanjikan)**

property **milik**

proud **bangga**; to be proud of **bangga pada**

provide, to (supply) **sedia (menyediakan)**; supply, stock **persediaan**

pull, to **tarik (menarik)**

pupil **murid**

put, to (place) **taruh (menaruh)**; (lay) **letak (meletakkan)**; put on, clothes **kena**

(mengenakan); (turn on, light) **pasang (memasang)**; put in **masuk (memasukkan)**

Q

queue **antri**

quiet, calm **tenang**; to quieten, calm down (transitive) **tenang (menenangkan)**; (noun) **ketenangan**

quite, rather **cukup**

R

rain **hujan**; to get caught in the rain **kehujanan**

rather, somewhat, a bit **agak**

reaction **réaksi**

ready **siap**

reasonable (makes sense) **masuk akal**; (not excessive) **lumayan**

receive, to **terima (menerima)**

recently **baru-baru ini**

recognize, to **kenal (mengenal)**

recover, to (get well) **sembuh**

red **mérah**

reduce, to **kurang (mengurangi)**; reduction **pengurangan**

refrigerator **lemari és**

regarding, about **akan/ tentang**

refuse, to (reject) **tolak (menolak)**; refusal, rejection **penolakan**

regular (regulated) **teratur**; (fixed) **tetap**; regularly **secara teratur**

religion **agama**

remember, to **ingat (mengingat)**; (be reminded of) **teringat**

remind, to (warn) **ingat (mengingati)**; (make think of) **mengingatkan**

remove, to (take away, out) **hilang (menghilangkan)**; remover **penghilang**; (to take off, clothes, shoes) **buka (membuka)**

repeatedly, time and again **berkali-kali**

reply, to (respond, reciprocate) **balas (membalas)**; (noun) **balasan**

report, to **lapor (melapor)**; (noun) **laporan**

reputation, good name **nama, nama baik**

request **permintaan**

request, to (invite) **sila (mempersilakan)**

research, to (investigate) **teliti (meneliti)**; (noun) **penelitian**

reservation, to make a reservation **memesan tempat**

respect, to **hormat (menghormati)**; (noun) **kehormatan**

respectful (greetings) **taklim/takzim**

responsible, to be **bertanggungjawab**

rest, break **istirahat**; to have a break **beristirahat**

result **akibat**

return, to (come, go back) **kembali**; (home) **pulang**; (noun) (ticket) **pergi-pulang**

rice (steamed) **nasi**; (uncooked) **beras**; (in field) **padi**; (plain cooked) **nasi putih**; (fried) **nasi goreng**

ricefield (irrigated) **sawah**

rich **kaya**; riches, wealth **kekayaan**

ride to ride in/on (car, motorcycle) **kendara (mengendarai)**

right (correct) **betul**

right (not left) **kanan**

rights **hak**; basic human rights **hak asasi manusia**

river **sungai**

road **jalan**; roadway **jalanan**; road sign **papan jalan**

role, part (in a play, etc.) **peranan**

room **kamar**; (large, e.g. hall) **ruang, ruangan**; single room **kamar untuk satu orang**; double room **kamar untuk dua orang**; (space) **tempat**

route, direction (of bus) **jurusan**

rural **pedésaan**

S

sad **sedih**; saddening **menyedihkan**

safe, secure **aman**; safety **keamanan**

salt **garam**

salty **asin**

same **sama**; of the same as **se-**; of the same opinion **sependapat**

sand **pasir**

sate **sate**

satisfied **puas**; satisfying **memuaskan**

sauce **saus**; soy sauce **kécap**; tomato sauce **saus tomat**

say, to (transitive) **kata (mengatakan)**; they say **katanya**

scared **takut**

scholarship **béasiswa**

school **sekolah**; primary school **sekolah dasar**; secondary school **sekolah menengah**; technical school **sekolah téknik**

science **ilmu**; scientific, scholarly **ilmiah**

sea **laut**

season **musim**; wet (rainy) season **musim hujan**; dry season **musim kering**

seat (in general) **tempat duduk**; (in bus, etc.) **tempat**

seatbelt **sabuk pengaman**

sedan (car) **sédan**

seldom, rarely **jarang**

self **diri**; oneself, of one's own **sendiri**

self-respect, self-esteem **harga diri**

sell, to **jual**; **menjual**

send, to **kirim (mengirim)**; something sent **kiriman**

serious (genuine) **betul-betul**; not joking **sérius**; (of problem, injury) **berat**

serve, to (at table) **layan**: **(melayani)**

shadow theatre **wayang kulit**

shake, to **gemetar**; to shake hands with **bersalaman dengan**

sharp **tajam**

shave, to **bercukur**; shaver, razor **alat cukur**

she **dia**; (respectful) **beliau**

ship **kapal**

shirt (men's) **keméja**; (general, also blouse) **baju**

shocked **kagét**; shocking **mengagétkan**

shop, store **toko**

short **péndék**

should **harus**

show, to **lihat (memperlihatkan)**

shower (bath) **dus**

sick **sakit**; sickness **penyakit**; travel sick **mabuk**

side (flank) **samping**; (left/right, point of compass) **sebelah**

side, edge **pinggir**

sign, indication, mark **tanda**; to put a sign, mark on something **tanda (menandai)**; there's no sign of (hasn't turned up) **belum muncul**

sign, to **téken**

signature **tandatangan**

signboard (on road) **papan jalan**; (with name) **papan nama**

simple, basic, modest **sederhana**; simplicity **kesederhanaan**

since (a time) **sejak**

sing, to **nyanyi (menyanyi)**; song **nyanyian**

Sir **Pak**

sister (younger) **adik**; (elder) **kakak** (add **perempuan** for "female" only if required)

sit, to **duduk**

situation **situasi**; (condition) **keadaan**

size, measurement **ukuran**

skirt **rok**

sky **langit**

sleep, to **tidur**

slice, to **iris (mengiris)**; (noun) **irisan**

slip, to (and fall) **keplését**

slope (of mountain) **léréng**

small **kecil**

smell (noun) **bau**; to smell (intransitive) **berbau**; (transitive) **cium (mencium)**

smile, to **tersenyum**; (noun) **senyum**

so (like that, to that extent) **begitu**; (consequently) **jadi**

so, so that (purpose) **supaya**

some (a few, several) **beberapa**; some time (in the future) **kapan-kapan**, **bésuk**

something **sesuatu**

sometimes **kadang-kadang**

son **anak laki-laki**; (of respected person) **putra**

soon (in a short time) **nanti**; (quickly) **lekas**

sore, to be **sakit**

sorry! **maaf!**

sort, kind **macam**

soul **jiwa**

sour **masam**

south **selatan**

space, room **tempat**

speak, to (talk) **bicara**; (use words) **berkata**

spectator, audience **penonton**

speed **kecepatan**

spit **ludah**; to spit **meludah**; to spit on **meludahi**

spoon **séndok**

sport **olahraga**

stall (for food, etc.) **warung**

stamp (postage) **perangko**

stand, to (of people) **berdiri**; (to be able to stand, tolerate) **tahan**

standpoint, opinion **pendirian**

starfruit, carambola **blimbing**

start, to (transitive) (get going, engine) **hidup (menghidupkan)**

startled **terkejut**

state, to **kata (mengatakan)**

state, nation **negara**

station (railway) **setasiun**; (bus) **términal bis**

steal, to **curi (mencuri)**

steps, to take steps **mengambil tindakan**

stiff (hard to bend, awkward) **kaku**; (wind) **kencang**

still (ongoing) **masih**; (unchanged) **tetap**

stone **batu**

stop, to (intransitive) **berhenti**; (transitive) **henti (menghentikan)**; stop! **setop!**; (noun) (bus) **halte**

story **cerita**

straight on **terus saja**

street **jalan**

struck, hit, on the spot **kena**

student (tertiary) **mahasiswa**; (secondary) **pelajar**

study, to (intransitive) **belajar**; (transitive) **mempelajari**; (noun) **pelajaran, studi**

suddenly **tiba-tiba**

sugar **gula**; palm sugar **gula kelapa/gula Jawa**

suggest, to **saran (menyarankan)**; suggestion **saran**

suitcase **kopor/koper**

sun **matahari**

sunbathe, to **berjemur diri**

sunburnt **kena sinar matahari**

superiors, bosses **atasan**

support, to (provide a living) **hidup (menghidupi)**

surname, family name **nama keluarga**

swallow, to **telan (menelan)**; swallowed accidentally **tertelan**

sweat (noun) **keringat**; to sweat **berkeringat**

sweet **manis**; (noun) **manisan**

sweets, hard lollies **kembang gula**

swim, to **berenang**; swimmer **perenang**; swimming costume **pakaian renang**; to go swimming **mandi** See also "bathe"

swimming pool **kolam renang**

symptom, sign **gejala**

T

table **méja**

take, to (away) **ambil (mengambil)**; (sugar) **pakai (memakai)**; (medicine) **minum**; (time) **makan waktu**; (leave) **minta diri**; (over) **mengambil alih**; (off, clothes, shoes) **buka (membuka)**; (to carry, take along) **bawa (membawa)**

takeoff **tinggal landas**

talk, to (chat) **omong (ngomong)**; (noun)

omong; idle talk
omong-omong

tally, to (fit, add up) **cocok**

tank (for splash bath) **bak mandi**; (for petrol) **téng bénsin**

taste, to (intransitive) **rasanya**; (transitive) **rasa (merasakan)**; (noun) **rasa**

tasty, delicious **énak**

taxi **taksi**

tea **téh**

teach, to (someone) **ajar (mengajar)**; (something) **mengajarkan**; teaching (noun) **pengajaran**

telephone, to **télépon (menélépon)**; telephone café **wartél**

temperature **suhu**

temple (ancient Javanese) **candi**; (Balinese) **pura**

ten **sepuluh**

tennis **ténis**; tennis player **peténis**

than **dari**

thank, to **mengucapkan terima kasih** (to: **kepada**, for: **atas**); thanks a lot **terima kasih banyak**; thank heavens! **syukurlah!**

that **itu**

that (introducing clause after verb of saying, thinking, etc.) **bahwa**

the mostly untranslated; sometimes the suffix **-nya** is used as a sort of definite article

then, after that **lalu**

there (in sight) **di situ**; (further away) **di sana**

they (people) **meréka**

thief **pencuri**

thing (object) **benda**; (matter, subject) **hal**

think, to (guess) **kira (mengira)**; (reflect) **berpikir**; to reflect about something **pikir (memikirkan)** *this* **ini**

thongs, flip-flops **sandal jepit**

thought (noun) **pikiran**

thousand **ribu**; one thousand **seribu**

throw, to **lémpar (melémpar)**; to throw at **melémpari**; to throw away **buang (membuang)**

ticket (airline) **tikét**; (bus, train, etc.) **karcis**

till, up to **sampai**

time **waktu**; (occasion) **kali**; the time being **sementara**; it's time to… **sudah waktunya untuk**; times gone by **témpo dulu**

timetable **jadwal**

tip (for waiter) **persén**

tired **capai** (pronounced capé, capék); tiring **melelahkan**; tired out, exhausted **kecapaian**

to (direction) **ke**; (giving, etc.) **kepada**; (towards, regarding) **terhadap**; (before, with times of day) **kurang**

today **hari ini**

toilet WC (pronounced wésé); to go to the toilet **ke belakang**; (more graphic) **membuang air**

tollroad **jalan tol**

tomato **tomat**

tomorrow **bésok**

tonight **malam ini**

too (also) **juga**; (excessively) **terlalu**

top **atas**

toward (regarding) **terhadap**; (in the direction of) **ke arah**

towel **anduk**

town **kota**

traffic **lalu lintas**

train **keréta api**

translate, to **terjemah (menerjemahkan)**; translation **terjemahan**

travel, to **berjalan**; to travel around **berkeliling**; (noun) **perjalanan**

traveller's cheque **travel cék**

tree **pohon**

true **benar**

truly **betul-betul**

trumpet **trompét**

trust, to **percaya pada**

try, to **coba (mencoba)**

T-shirt **kaos**

turn, to (intransitive) **bélok**; to turn off (light) **mati (mematikan)**

twice **dua kali**

U

umbrella **paying**

unbearable **tidak tertahan lagi**

uncle **paman**; (Westerner) **om**

understand, to **mengerti**; understanding (noun) **pengertian**

unfortunately, it's a pity that … **sayangnya**

university **univérsitas**

unmarried (male) **bujangan**

until **sampai**

up (to the top) **ke atas**; up to (until) **sampai**; it's up to you **terserah**

urine, to urinate **kencing**

us **kita** (inclusive of you); **kami** (exclusive of you)

use, to **pakai (memakai)**

used to, accustomed **biasa**

useful **berguna**

usual **biasa**; usually **biasanya**

V

vacant **lowong**; vacancy (job) **lowongan**

valid **sah**

value, to **harga (menghargai)**

valuable **berharga**

vanish, to **hilang (menghilang)**

very **sekali** (following); **sangat** (preceding word concerned)

via (through, by way of) **léwat**

view, to (consider) **pandang (memandang)**; (noun) (opinion) **pandangan**

view, scenery **pemandangan**

village **désa**

violation, transgression **pelanggaran**

visa **visa**

visit, to (go on a visit to) **berkunjung ke**;

(transitive) **kunjung (mengunjungi)**; (noun) **kunjungan**; visitor **pengunjung**

volleyball **voli**; volleyball player **pemain voli**

W

wait, to **tunggu (menunggu)**

waiter **pelayan**

walk, to (go on foot) **berjalan kaki**; to go for a walk **berjalan-jalan**

wall (of brick, etc.) **témbok**

want, to **mau**

warm (welcome, clothes) **hangat**; (weather, climate) **panas**

wash, to **cuci (mencuci)**; washing (noun) (clothes to be washed) **cucian**; (drying in sun) **jemuran**

washbasin **wastafel**

watch, to (for entertainment) **tonton**

(menonton); watch over, look after **tunggu (menunggu)**

watch (wristwatch) **jam tangan**

water **air**; plain water **air putih**; for bathing **air mandi**

waterfall **air terjun**

watermelon **semangka**

wave, to **melambaikan tangan**

wave (in sea) **ombak**

way (path) **jalan**; (roadway) **jalanan**; (method, custom) **cara**; in a … way **secara**; on the way **dalam perjalanan**

we **kita** (inclusive of you); **kami** (exclusive of you)

wear, to (clothes) **pakai (memakai)**

weather **cuaca**

wedding **perkawinan**

week **minggu**

welcome, you're **kembali!**; to welcome **sambut (menyambut)**; (noun) **sambutan**

well **baik-baik**; (healthy) **séhat**; (noun) (for water) **sumur**

west **barat**; the West **Barat**; Westerner **orang Barat**

wet **basah**; sopping wet **basah kuyup**; wet season **musim hujan**

what? **apa?**; what kind of **macam apa?**; what (is it, etc.) like? **bagai-mana?**; what about … **bagaimana …**

when **kapan?** when (in the past) **waktu**; (if) **kalau**

where? **di mana?** (to where?) **ke mana?**

whether **apakah**

which (which one?) **yang mana**; (relative pronoun: which, who, that) **yang** *whistle, to* **bersiul**

white **putih**

who? **siapa?**

whole **seluruh**; the whole of it **seluruhnya**

wicked, bad, evil **jahat**; wickedness **kejahatan**

wide **lébar**

wife **isteri**

will (going to) **akan**

wind **angin**

window **jendéla**; (for selling tickets) **lokét**

wish, to (want, desire) **ingin**

wishes, best **mengucapkan selamat**

with **dengan**

within **dalam**

without **tanpa**

witness, to **saksi (menyaksikan)**

wonder, to (keep asking oneself) **tertanya-tanya**; (want to know) **ingin tahu**

wonder, no wonder, of course, indeed **mémang**

word **kata, perkataan**

work, to **bekerja**; to work on (transitive) **kerja (mengerjakan)**; (noun) (general) **kerja**, (job) **pekerjaan**; worker **pekerja**

worker (labourer) **buruh**; the workers **kaum buruh**

write, to **tulis (menulis)**; writing (noun) **tulisan**; written **tertulis**

wrong, mistaken, at fault **salah**

Y

year **tahun**

yellow **kuning**

yet, not yet **belum**; (nevertheless) **namun**

you (familiar) **kamu**;
(polite) **anda**; (formal)
saudara

young **muda**

your (familiar) **mu**;
(polite) **anda**; (formal)
saudara (placed after
the object possessed)

youth, the **kaum muda**